# WORDS THOUGHT AND SAID:
# PRAYERS AND REFLECTIONS

W.J.G. McDonald

Handsel Press

© W.J.G. McDonald 2014

Published by

Handsel Press

35 Dunbar Rd

Haddington

EH41 3PJ

Scotland

ISBN 978-1-871828-81-8

Cover Design, Typesetting and Layout by: Sanctus Media Ltd
Printed by: The Printing House, London
Front Cover Photograph: Roddy Martine
Front Cover Image: Detail from apse window at Mayfield Salisbury Church
Back Cover Photograph: courtesy of The Scotsman Newspaper Group

# Contents

## — SERMONS —

## — THOUGHTS FOR THE DAY —

WORDS THOUGHT AND SAID: PRAYERS AND REFLECTIONS

W.J.G. McDonald

## *Note on the Author*

Bill McDonald, the Very Revd Dr William James Gilmour McDonald, graduated from the University of Edinburgh with a starred First in Classics. His first job was that of wartime gunner, as a captain with a Punjabi Musulman battery in an Indian Army anti-tank regiment. After training at New College, he became a parish minister, initially in Fife and then, for over 30 years, at Mayfield Church in Edinburgh. He served as Moderator of the General Assembly of the Church of Scotland in 1989/90. He was awarded an honorary Doctor of Divinity degree by the University of Edinburgh in 1987.

# Foreword

## by David Fergusson

In 1979–80 during my final year as a Divinity student in Edinburgh, I was privileged to serve as student assistant at Mayfield Church. Attending morning and evening worship conducted by Bill McDonald, I came to appreciate the high quality and consistency of his work. Eschewing the oratorical fireworks of previous generations of ministers, he preached in a lively conversational manner and drew upon contemporary expressions and images in the language of his prayers. The effect was profound. Allied to his keen observation of everyday life was an intellectual acumen, felicity of expression and steady devotion to the traditions of the Christian faith. Though shy by temperament, he could mesmerize a large congregation and leave a lasting impression.

More than thirty years later, I can still remember some of his sermons and turns of phrase. These had an enduring impact, and I recall James Whyte, his friend and predecessor at Mayfield, once likening his services to a wine with a memorable aftertaste. Bill made me realize that it was possible to be simultaneously orthodox and contemporary, liberal and evangelical, colloquial yet dignified in expression. These qualities provided the ideal combination for some of the most effective Thoughts for the Day that BBC Scotland has delivered.

Several of his prayers found their way into Common Order (1994). While unattributed, they are now regularly used and appreciated at services throughout the Church of Scotland. This wider selection of material has been gathered in the hope that it will be of further benefit to public worship and private devotion. Readers are free to adapt and recycle these prayers and reflections in whatever ways they wish. And some, whose lives were nourished by Bill's long ministry at Mayfield Salisbury Church, can gratefully recall the worship he conducted over many years.

I am grateful to Jean Reynolds, Frances Henderson and Nicola Whyte at New College for their assistance in editing and transcribing material, to the Hope Trust for underwriting the costs of publication, and to Neil MacLennan at

Sanctus Media for his work in the copy-editing and publishing of the volume. Special thanks are owed to Sheena McDonald for her assistance with the selection of materials as well as her support, advice and encouragement throughout this project. And finally we are indebted to Roddy Martine for his photograph of the detail from the apse window at Mayfield Salisbury Church, Edinburgh. The lion symbolizes Mark's Gospel, the earliest and shortest of the four stories of Jesus' life.

# Introduction

## WORDS THOUGHT AND SAID

### by Bill McDonald

One of the most influential writers in Scotland was the poet William Soutar, who was confined to bed, beside a window, for most of his his later life. He died at 45. As well as writing poems, he kept a journal, which is treasured by many people. In it, he wrote this: 'Silence is perhaps the greatest hallelujah; the silent hosannas of the sun, the stars, the trees and the flowers . . . but silence is not enough – the innumerable songs of earth mingle – the winds, the water, the cries of bird and beast and the thoughtful utterances of humanity.'

A large part of my life as a minister has been spent attempting to compose and deliver 'thoughtful utterances' in the form of prayers and sermons, a weekly job for every preacher, and one which requires a combination of understanding and ingenuity. This book offers suggestions on how to do the job.

How does one write sermons and prayers? The task requires establishing a relationship with the listener – finding the same wavelength, as it were. Any kind of public speaking requires one to find some common ground with the listener – and this must come before activating the mechanisms of composition, so that the listener doesn't feel that he or she is being manipulated via techniques used by someone alien, but shares thoughts and feelings with the speaker.

The tools I have used are simple. For the first half of my 30-plus years as a parish minister, I relied on a portable typewriter that I had 'liberated' from Java in 1946. I was an officer in a Punjabi Musulman battery of an Indian Army anti-tank regiment. One day, I saw by the roadside this typewriter lying upside-down, and some yards away the cover for it. I tossed both into my 15cwt. truck. They came home with me in my Bergen rucksack as my one souvenir. It was my only typewriter until the late 1970s, to the astonishment of visiting ministers who could not believe that this antiquated pre-war Dutch Continental machine, which had a sign for the guilder and one for the letter 'ij', should be the only mechanical aid that the minister of a reasonably important church possessed – but it was.

The other essential tool is the Bible, in whatever version one chooses.

And so to the thoughtful utterances – what words or thoughts can better a great hallelujah of silence? The late composer John Tavener spoke eloquently about trying to find "a music that already exists in the cosmos" or "the uncreated music of God".

Is a preacher attempting something complementary – finding and using words that express God's purpose and love?

The challenge for the speaker or preacher is to try to find words and ideas that the listener will identify with, that reflect the uncertainty of the listener in terms of the anxieties and hopes that form a bridge of communication between the speaker and the unknown listener – whose response to what he or she hears will reflect the limitations of the speaker. Jesus spoke to people, but he knew well enough that often people were not really hearing what he was saying. Listening perhaps but not hearing. He used to say, 'Those who have ears to hear, let them hear.' And he still speaks. The Christian man or woman has a duty to keep their ears open – not to hear only the voice of self-interest but the voice of the neighbour, wherever or whoever that neighbour may be. God speaks not just through the prophets of old, but through the cry of a hungry child, the scream of a tortured prisoner, in the unheard speech of the one shut away, forgotten by many people but not forgotten by God. And in the voices of the natural order that we are part of, the song of the birds, heard less and less in our industrialised world, the strange speech of whales communicating in terms we do not understand, the wind in the great trees that we cannot create though we can so easily destroy them forever.

So the preacher's task is to find those words that let in the light and sound, and help people to listen and hear. We need to remember the words "Be still and know that I am God" – God who, whatever tradition or religion we may belong to, is heard in the still small voice of silence. And then to be not hearers of the word only, but do-ers of it. God speaks, and listening to that voice, new life the dead receive, new life and work to do – all of us in obedience to God, and to the service of God's world.

# — PRAYERS —

# PRAYERS OF APPROACH AND CONFESSION

1.  Lord, this we believe:
    that in a world where there are kings and queens,
    and presidents and emperors,
    and governments and parties,
    you ultimately are the King.

    Lord, this we believe:
    that in a word where there are parents and leaders,
    and teachers and advisors and personalities,
    you above all are Father to us.

    Lord, this we believe:
    that in a world where there are so many people offering to help,
    so many people who make things difficult,
    where there are so many people making demands on us,
    and asking help from us,
    where there are so many people,
    you are our helper and our strength.

    Lord, this we believe:
    that in a world that has power to destroy itself,
    in a world where there is enough food but not enough concern,
    enough fuel but not enough self-discipline,
    enough knowledge but not enough love,
    you are the one who can give meaning to our lives,
    and purpose and a future for all.

    Each of us is known to you,
    what we have done and what we should do,
    and what we could be.
    Forgive the many things that we have done wrong.
    Help us to live as your sons and daughters,
    to know Jesus Christ,
    and to follow him all the way.

2. Father, we offer our selves before you by name,
all of us known, uniquely fingerprinted, each uniquely created,
genetically coded in your great book of life,
our lives unlike any individual life that has ever existed,
our path this week following a course
that will not be matched by other persons.

Yet our pilgrimage is such as others have made countless times.
We are not the first to be tempted to be slothful and selfish,
not the first to have succumbed in the past
to the temptations of the flesh and of the spirit,
not the first to have asked for forgiveness,
to have repented, and then to have fallen again.
Father you have heard it all before, from us and from millions of others.
But unlike us, many others having fallen as we have fallen, have risen to
newness of life, to victorious Christian living, to lives of heroism and service
and sacrifice, not through their own power but through the power of Christ.
Father we know our own weakness, the low threshold of attainment that we
can reach, but with you all things are possible.
Give us not only true penitence, not only full forgiveness, but power
sufficient to rise and to live again, to be more than conquerors through
Jesus Christ our Lord.

Help us, Lord, to worship as we should now, not any more to dwell upon
ourselves and our own needs and failures; but to contemplate and reflect
upon the glory and beauty of our Lord Christ, that we may be drawn to him,
that we may go out to serve and follow him.
We are called to be soldiers, however timorous we may be.
We are called to be ambassadors, however gauche or unacceptable or
inarticulate we may believe ourselves to be.
We are called to be evangelists however conscious we may be of how our
lives hitherto would belie our words.
Give us the quality of life that will make our words convincing,
give us that strange thing which is inward peace,
that we may not fear the future nor ask too many questions about it,
that we may sleep well at night, work hard during the day, and find
enjoyment in our time of relaxation and refreshment,
that we may in all we do be pleasing to you our God.

3. Living and eternal God, accept the prayers and the love of us your people, of us your children. For you are our Father, whose arms are open to us, whose hand is ever ready to take hold of ours, who, when our bodies are tired, and our hearts are cold, takes us and cherishes us to yourself.

Receive us now, Lord, just as we are, aware of so many things we have failed to do that we should have done, of so many things that we have done that would have been better not done, so much that we regret.
Some of these things we confess now, and we ask for forgiveness for them, so that we may be able to pray again, and to believe again and to serve you as you deserve.

Father, you have given us so much and so generously; you have shown your love to us in giving Jesus Christ to be our Saviour and Lord.
Help us Lord to love you better, to serve you more faithfully, to be the sort of people we want to be and that we believe you want us to be.

4. Loving God, generous Father, omnipotent Lord,
from the richness and distractions of our world we come to you,
to share with you our fears, our joys, our frailties,
our tiredness, our hopes and expectations, our thanksgivings.

From being at other times strong and mature and competent,
we come to admit to you our weakness.

From being at times forgotten, expendable and of little account in the world,
we come to you to rejoice in our value, we believe, in your sight.

From failure and sin and faithlessness,
we come to be made clean and new again.

From being on our own
we come to share in our oneness with one another in your sight.

As disobedient children,
as rebellious sons and daughters,

as disloyal subjects,
as creatures who have much to discover about the purpose of our being here,
we come for wisdom and direction,
for clarity of vision, where so much is obscure,
for grace to bow before the presence of the mystery,
where so much seems so obvious.
So that we may be free to weep, and to laugh, and to sing, and to live,
so we come, O God.

We thank you for all the people who have gone before us in the faith, people
we know ourselves and the millions we cannot know but who in their lives
proved that Christ could save and keep and strengthen and bless.
In our worship be near to us, in our daily lives help us to walk with Christ.


5. O Lord our God, whose grace and mercy have come near in Jesus Christ
your Son, we ascribe glory to you, king of glory, God of grace.

Most merciful Father,
who at the first made the world to be fair and good,
whose love for it has never changed,
who sealed your creation as your own by the death of Jesus Christ;
we who have our own part within your creation,
and within your love,
and within the reconciliation of all things wrought by him for us,
would offer our adoring worship and praise to you.

With all your creation we have fallen from this obedience,
with less excuse than others,
for we have known that you gave Jesus Christ to be Saviour and Lord,
and yet we have sinned against you and against your love.

We bless you for the grace that is sufficient to cover all our sin,
for the pardon freely bestowed on all who claim cleansing and newness of
life in Jesus Christ.

O Lord God assist our worship that we may give our minds to meditation upon your word and upon your love.

May the grace shown in the coming of your son and in the cross of Calvary, in the empty tomb and in the continuing life of the church be constant in our lives.


6.  Worship the Lord in the beauty of holiness.

Father, this is our worship:
to turn away from daily duties and the passing show,
and from work that awaits us tomorrow;
to stand in the presence of what is real,
to bow in the presence of the Eternal.

Father, this is our worship:
to come running,
to tell out before we forget it all that has befallen us,
what we have done and achieved and enjoyed,
to share it with one who knows it all and understands it all.

Father, this is our worship:
to unburden our hearts of the things that we are ashamed of;
things done and thought and said; things left undone too.
To admit to what others would be surprised to know and shocked to know,
and the desperate unbelief that takes possession of us and makes mockery
of our insecurities and of our pretensions.
For with you alone is forgiveness.
You alone can show us who you are and what our lives are for.

Father, this is our worship:
to give expression to our hopes and desires,
that others might find amusing or pathetic,
the inmost aspirations and goals that we still hold before ourselves,
not for fantasizing but for true fulfillment.

Father, this is our worship:
not to speak too much,
to listen more than we usually do,
to reflect, to accept, and to resolve.

Father, this is our worship:
to see Jesus,
to be touched by him,
to come to our feet and rise up and follow him.

Father, this is our worship – we offer it to you.


7. Father eternal, by whom we judge what human parenthood should be:
   wise and just, strong and fair,
   with time for your children,
   kind to them and generous, and more loving than they know,
   agonizing over them while they sleep,
   caring for them in ways that they take for granted.
   As children we come, all of us, before you,
   fearful sometimes,
   rebellious too often,
   full of joy and trust and confidence
   when we remember who you are and what you are.

   We put our hands into yours again, asking for things which only love could
   grant and only greater wisdom than ours might withhold.
   Today forgive what we have been and still are,
   teach us to trust you, show us how to live.
   Give us confidence to speak to you often
   and to desire to walk in the light of your presence.
   Hear the prayers that we say and the prayers we dare not utter.

   Help us, O God, to offer our due worship to you now, and consciously to
   serve you for the rest of this day and in all our tomorrows.
   For Jesus' sake.

8.  Seven days, O God, is in our sight a long time.
    But we would try to gather up the week's endeavours in your sight
    and in our remembrance,
    And to do so in thanksgiving and in penitence:
    Things done corporately here,
    Or in the name of this congregation elsewhere;
    Prayers offered, duties performed,
    Acts of service undertaken;
    The life of home, of business, of family, of community.

    And now today, as we are, we come back,
    to have our batteries recharged,
    our vision refocused,
    the tired muscles of the spirit
    massaged into shape again.
    forgive us that we have not lived up
    to what we have been called to be.
    set our sights higher than they were,
    that we may aim bravely,
    and by the Spirit's direction may attain.
    make us simpler people than we are;
    more passionate in our loving,
    more committed in our caring,
    less inhibited in our enjoying,
    more vulnerable in our understanding
    of the suffering of others,
    more courageous in our own,
    more pure in heart than we are –
    that we may yet see God.
    Through Jesus Christ our Lord.

    Glory be to you O God the Father Almighty, maker of heaven and earth,
    of whose faithfulness there is no end.
    Glory be to you, O Lord Jesus Christ,
    the Saviour of the world,
    who by your cross and precious blood has redeemed us.
    Glory be to you, O God the Holy Spirit,

the Lord and giver of life
who takes the things of Christ and show them unto us.
O holy and eternal God,
Father, Son and Holy Spirit,
to you we ascribe all blessing and honour and glory, now and for ever.

9. O God, look upon us who would now seek to offer you,
   as best we may, the pure and devout worship of our hearts.
   Speak to us as we offer you our hymns and praises, our prayers, our gifts.
   Speak through your word, speak through the silence.

   We come to you to affirm our fellowship anew with one another,
   and with you.

   We come for cleansing. You see and know us, and yet love us; and you hold
   out pardon and renewal in Jesus Christ who was made sin for us that our
   sins might be done away.
   So grant us cleansing.

   We come for confession, for we have all forsaken you, have served you
   amiss, and have sinned against your holy love.
   So hear us as for our healing we confess to you.

   We come for comfort, for without you we are weak and frail yet we believe
   that through the indwelling Christ we can do all things.
   Strengthen us, O God, with might by your Spirit within.

   We come to you, O God, for commissioning. You have made us for yourself.
   Sanctify our doings as a congregation, make every home a church, and
   every heart a consecrated dwelling of yours.

   Almighty God, in whom men and women find their life,
   you have so made us that our lives are not complete without you, or satisfied
   or at peace apart from you; you have implanted in us the desire for you and
   the need for you. In this place of prayer we seek you.

10. O God we are tormented in our perverseness.
    We fear you and we love you.
    We flee from you and yearn for you.
    We repent our sins, and then we go back and sin.
    We ask newness of life, and then we return to what we have been.
    We catch a glimpse of glory and beauty, and then we shrug it away.
    We ask many things in our prayers; we like the sound of the words, but we do not overmuch want our prayers to be answered.
    We believe, but we do not seriously believe.
    We ask to be accepted as we are, but we do not want to be changed.
    We know you will not change us against our will, and we are content with that. We are happy with our failings, and we do not much mind our sins.
    There is no health or consistency in us.
    We are not worthy of love, for we have compromised love, and tarnished love. And we are not worthy of the cross of Christ – for it was our sin that caused it, our frailty that pierced and wounded a Lord who yet cares.
    Deliver us from evil.
    Enable us to rise to the stature of what we are called to become.
    Give us power to lift our eyes to your face, to see what love is, and what love costs, and what love demands, and what love offers, so that we may as children find love and confidence and light in your presence.


11. Gracious Father,
    loving God,
    as children of a day we come to the eternal Lord.
    Ignorant and heedless creatures,
    we come to the ultimate wisdom.
    Convicted sinners,
    we kneel before the judge.
    Penitent sinners,
    we turn our eyes to the one who alone can forgive.

    We who have worked too little at our calling as disciples, messengers, interpreters, doers of the faith, come back to be sent out once again.
    We who have taken early retirement from the high endeavour with which once we set our hands to the plough, with which we enlisted and took

upon us the whole armour of God, ask to be given another chance to prove ourselves,
to demonstrate our love and our willingness to bear hardship and to share in the victory.

More than all else now, we gather to offer worship and praise for so many things in our own lives,
in the life of our country,
in the tradition we have inherited.
We have lost count of our blessings, or we have not for a long time dared to count them, let alone to name them and confess them;
The things that some of us would want to name in a word before you.

Grant to us such penitence,
such thankfulness,
such confidence in a love that is greater than all our failure and all our sin,
such trust in the merits of Jesus Christ, that, ransomed, healed, restored, and forgiven, we may again rise up and follow him, for his love's sake.

12. The earth belongs to the Lord.
You belong to Christ. Draw near to God. Let us pray.

Mighty and merciful God,
from everlasting to everlasting creator and redeemer,
lover of your creation and of us creatures within it,
quieten our hearts to worship,
to see,
to ponder,
to adore.
We have so many requests to make to you, but we doubt our wisdom that would let us ask with confidence.
Our lives are tainted by our part in the whole life of the world around us.
We have denied and doubted love, and our own lives have been stunted and impoverished thereby.

We have not cared for our neighbours as we ought,
have not helped them,
nor prayed for them,
given time to them,
suffered with them.
We have admired Jesus Christ yet have not followed him,
nor truly loved him.
For these our common sins, and for certain sins particular to each of us,
we ask forgiveness.
From these sins, we ask deliverance, for Jesus' sake whose death was related
to our sinfulness and is the cure for it.
Members of the church and of one another, we come for grace that in us the
church may be strong and not weak, and the world be more wholesome and
happy because of our commitment to its life and wellbeing.
Make us followers of Jesus Christ.


13. Eternal and living God, giver of this day and of all the days,
creator of many worlds and of this world, acknowledged by so many millions
of people in every generation, and worshipped now by ourselves:
The more we think of you, the more confused we often are,
but in the face of Jesus Christ we have seen your face,
in his love we see your love,
his grace and mercy to us are your grace and mercy,
in your love we find our confidence and our hope.
Father we are not strong for you as we ought to be:
our trust wavers,
our own love grows cold,
we have not shone as lights in the world,
or made Christian faith in you compelling and desirable for others.
But you are our Father, and we believe;
help us Father in our unbelief.
Together, Lord, we could do unimaginable things for you,
creating a community where the young would grow up in security and the
old would not be afraid.
Even one by one we could find meaning for all our lives and help others to
find meaning for theirs too.

14. Jesus said, "Come and eat."
    And none of the disciples dared ask him, "Who are you?"
    They knew it was the Lord.

    He satisfies the longing soul, and fills the hungry soul with goodness.

    Almighty God, to whom all hearts be open, all desires known, and from whom no secrets are hid, cleanse the thoughts of our hearts by the inspiration of your Holy Spirit, that we may perfectly love you and worthily magnify your holy name, through Jesus Christ our Lord.

    Almighty God, who so loved the world as to give your only begotten Son that whoever believes in him shall not die, but have eternal life, in his name who offered himself a sacrifice on our behalf, who bore our sins in his own body on the tree, we adore you.

    Our sins cry out against us, but you are greater than our sins. We have failed you, we have gone our own way, we have been neither good soldiers nor good ambassadors of Jesus Christ. From our shame and our sin, aware of the coldness of our hearts and of our need for you, we offer ourselves to you. Have mercy upon us, restore us.

    O God, who has prepared for them that love you such good things as pass our understanding, pour into our hearts such love towards you that we, loving you above all things, may obtain your promises which exceed all that we can desire, through Jesus Christ our Lord, to whom with you and the Holy Spirit be all honour and glory, world without end.

    Make us want these things to happen, and then equip us, Lord, accordingly.
    Make us clean again, as perhaps once we were,
    help us to believe as perhaps once we did,
    or as we have never yet succeeded in doing.
    Gather us together at your table and feed our souls and spirits.
    Help us with seriousness and with joy to celebrate this day.

15. Lord God, look upon this company of people, this extended family claiming
relation with one another because you are Father to us all.
Do for us what we expect a good father to do.
Open your arms to us, forgive us the things for which we are sorry, explain
to us the things by which we are perplexed, advise us what we are to do.
Give us confidence again and cheerfulness and hope.
Hear our songs and our quiet prayers.
In your word and sacrament come near to us, O God,
through Jesus Christ our Lord.

16. In the light of what we have seen and heard, we confess, O God, that we
have not fully grasped or entered into the meaning of these days.
Forgive us, O God, who have so often gone our own way, when a living Lord
was at hand to lead and guide.
Forgive us, O God, who have so often struggled on in our own strength,
when all the resources of eternity were available through faith.
Forgive us, O God, who have been so slow to believe, so slow to obey.
Forgive us, O God, who have refused the comfort of him who has conquered
death, and the daily help of him who has conquered sin.
Forgive us that we have been cast down and dismayed by the changes and
chances of this world, when our Saviour Christ has overcome the world.

Speak to our hearts the words that will declare forgiveness for sins past,
strength in temptation yet to come, and purpose in the days lying before us.
Lord Jesus, stand among us in your risen power, and be known to us in
your mercy and grace.

And to you who with the Father everlasting and the Spirit of life now live
and reign for ever, we shall ascribe all glory on this day and forever.

17. I am certain of this: neither death nor life, no angel, no prince, nothing
that exists, nothing still to come, not any power, or height or depth, nor any
created thing, can ever come between us and the love of God made visible
in Christ Jesus our Lord.

Lord God almighty, we give thanks for our freedom overnight from flood and hurricane,
from bombing and violence,
from hunger and illness and desolation.
Who are we, O God, to be spared what so many have suffered?

We give thanks that amid the fears of our day,
our world still stands firm,
we have those to whom to turn,
that our faith still stands sure,
that our Lord stands sovereign over the flood,
that Jesus Christ is the same yesterday, today and forever.
And so we meet, humbly, gratefully, confidently.

We have sinned, O God.
We have sinned against you, our God.
We have let you down.
We have let down other people who looked to us, we have not loved them enough or helped them enough.
We have not even been true to ourselves and what we most believe.
We know that others have failed us too, and disappointed us.
But we would seek now grace once and for all to forgive those who have sinned against us,
and we intend to be reconciled and to make it up with those with whom we are at odds.
Because this is our intention, we ask that you will forgive our sins, O God,
that there may be no barrier between our God and ourselves.
For Jesus died to break down such walls of separation.

Give us reality now in what we say and think and resolve.
Make us more like what we are meant to be,
wiser,
happier,
less selfish,
with better vision and deeper faith.

18. The heavens declare your glory, O God, and our voices would not be silent.
Not casually would we offer praise, but fullbloodedly.
Not as of duty or routine would we ascribe glory and honour to you, our
Father, but from the depth of our being,
from the living depth of our hearts.

Not conventionally would we confess sin committed,
duty undone,
penitence and regret unexperienced,
joy and sorrow unexplored,
sacrifice for Christ's sake not accepted,
pain not absorbed for the suffering of the world.

Lord, break the shell of our conventional piety, and of our routine worship.
Come to us in love,
that we may not flinch from your love's embrace,
nor decline your forgiveness,
nor be deaf to your calling of us once again.

Lord, we have no original sins to confess, but only such as have tarnished
the lives and weakened the witness of so many others before us.
But we know that unless we confess, even the things that we are ashamed
to confess,
we cannot be forgiven,
that unless we are reconciled to our neighbour and to one another,
we cannot be reconciled to you.

So hear the sins that now silently we name; hear the names of those with
whom we intend to be reconciled . . .

We do this in the name of Jesus Christ, our Lord.

19. This is the boldness which we have toward you, O God:
    that if we ask anything according to your will, you hear us.
    And we know that your Spirit helps our weakness,
    because we know not what we should pray for.
    So help us therefore, O Lord, to draw near with boldness to your throne of
    grace that we may receive mercy and find grace to help us in time of need.

    Where you are, O Lord, there is peace,
    in every storm and tumult, there is peace when your word is spoken.
    And when hopes are fading and faith wavers, your word provides the sure
    strength that we need.
    And when our sin rises up before us and we know our guiltiness in your
    sight, then it is only your word of forgiveness that can lift us up and make
    us clean and whole again.

    We would confess to you, O Lord, the sins which have marred our life and
    spoiled our witness.
    You know how far short we have come even of our own standards.
    You know the faithlessness, the prayerlessness, that have weakened our
    spirits. You know how seldom we have spoken for you and how our practice
    has come short even of that which we have professed.
    O Lord God, who has planted us in this world to be courageous and faithful
    servants of yours,
    and has bidden us to be strong and of a good courage,
    renew our spirits we pray,
    forgive those sins that we have committed,
    and having forgiven them blot them out,
    that forgetting those things which are behind,
    we may press on to the goal to which you call us,
    even likeness to Jesus Christ,
    to whom with you, O Father, and the Holy Spirit be all honour and glory,
    now and for ever.

20. O holy Lord God, who searches the hearts of all people,
    cleanse us from all hypocrisy,
    and open our hearts that we may both know the truth and do it,
    through Christ our Lord.

    Father in heaven, who has granted us a father's blessing,
    supplying all our needs, of body and of mind and of spirit,
    we give you thanks that you know us so much better than we know ourselves,
    and that you not only answer our prayers before we utter them,
    but that you provide abundantly for needs of ours before we knew what our
    needs are.
    For the love that cared for us from our earliest days when we knew nothing
    of it,
    for the self-sacrifice of loved ones and the kindness of friends that we did
    nothing to merit,
    for the Holy Scriptures which lay to our hand as a guide,
    for the heritage of faith and devotion through many generations into which
    we entered in the Church,
    and most of all that when we knew our rebellion and the sin in which we
    stood and were powerless to redeem ourselves, we found a redemption,
    the Lamb of God, slain from the foundation of the world.

    For these and all your mercies,
    which have gone before us every step of the way,
    and which we trust will never fail,
    we thank and bless you, O Lord our God, in Jesus' name.

21. O God, you have made all things: the infinitely great, and the infinitely tiny.
    You have made us, in a strange and wonderful manner.

    We give thanks for our bodies – the living machines, the hearts that beat
    unceasing and unresting.
    For our senses, that we can see beauty, and need.
    For the taste of what is for our health and nourishment.
    For the scent of flowers.
    For the touch of hands, and of rock, and the texture of what is good to touch.

That we can hear music and birdsong, and the cry of the helpless.
Help us to use our bodies well. Forgive us for our sins against them: through fatigue, through negligence, through lust, through sloth, through indulgence, through greed.
Help us to honour them as temples of the Spirit.

We give thanks for our minds.
For what quickens them to action.
For the disciplines of our work.
For the happiness of memory.
For the excitement of imagination.
Help us to use our minds well.
Forgive us for lethargy of thinking.
For when we allow others to do our thinking for us.
For prejudice and complacency, and the clichés in which we so easily think.
For the closed mind.
Help us to furnish our minds and fill them with what is good, that they may be places of light and honour.

We give thanks for our spirits.
For human love and the dimensions it opens up to us.
For the timeless blessings of beauty and joy.
For the light of the Gospel calling us to new adventures of living, of faith, of commitment.
Forgive us for spirits dim and lifeless and gloomy.
For spirits that give too small a place to your Spirit, or to Jesus Christ.
Help us to honour our spirits, to keep them bright and clear.
Give us the radiant spirit, hearts filled with joy and love and peace.
Take possession of us – of our bodies, a living sacrifice, holy and acceptable to you; of our minds, that the mind which was in Christ Jesus may be in our minds; of our spirits, that they may be constantly renewed by your love, and that eternal life may have its dwelling there, that we may belong to you forever.

22. "The earth is the Lord's, and all that is in it." (Psalm 24:1a)

"Happy is the nation whose God is the Lord." (Psalm 23:12a)

"Unless the Lord guards the city the guard keeps watch in vain."
(Psalm 127:1b)

Lord God, who has given us such a goodly heritage in this land,
we praise you,
Lord of lords, King of kings,
for all that we have neither earned nor deserved.

For your grace to us in our birth,
our place within the minority of those who live in freedom,
of those who live in comfort,
of those who live with sufficiency of food and shelter and clothing,
for this land,
the justice of its laws and its government,
the many freedoms we possess within it,
we bless you.

For your grace to us in our redemption,
For the faith in which we were nurtured,
the church in which we were reared,
the Bible that lay to our hand,
the infinitely good gifts of your grace,
our worship,
our fellowship,
the Gospel we have received,
the Gospel of which you have made us heralds.
For these we bless you.

Forbid, O Lord, that we should exalt ourselves that we are not as other
people are, in that you have given us so much, knowing that to whom much
is given, of him will the more be required.

We acknowledge our debts, O God, which we have not and cannot ever repay. Forgive our debts as we forgive our debtors,
our debts of gratitude and devotion and service,
that not out of duty but out of utter thankfulness we may offer you the service of our lives.

Make us stewards of our wealth.
Make us good ambassadors of the word you have entrusted to us all.
We ask that our churches and our homes reflect and commend your goodness.

# ADVENT

Almighty God, who did not turn from the sin of the world,
grant to your church to take seriously the incarnation of your Son,
to set forth his claims and his glory,
to call us to penitence at this season for the humiliation and sufferings of Christ,
and to holy thanksgiving that though he was rich,
yet for our sakes he became poor and laid aside his glory.
And grant to her so to enter into the life of the world as he entered,
that in the world of the home, where he lived,
in the world of industry where he laboured,
and in the sufferings of humanity which he also suffered,
she may also spend and be spent,
she may seek no greater glory than was his,
desire no greater splendour than he knew,
and covet no higher destiny than he embraced who gave himself to the uttermost in love.

O Lord Jesus Christ, who is our peace,
who broke down the middle wall of partition to unite those who otherwise had no way of reconciliation,
we ask that you will reconcile men and women,
and hasten the fulfilment of your Kingdom.

O Lord Jesus Christ who bid us observe the duties of nationality,
we pray for this nation,
for the sovereign, for the Prime Minister, and for all who govern us.

O Lord Jesus Christ, who in the mystery of your love became a little child,
we pray for all children, especially such as are homeless or who have lost
parents, that the beauty and wonder of Christmastime may so encompass
their lives as to abide with them in simplicity and joy all their days.

O Lord Jesus Christ, who toiled and laboured in the world's work,
we commend to you those who doubt the concern of God in the conditions
of their daily life,
that whatever the response of human beings to them,
they may know their world sanctified by yours,
and may find in work a vocation and privilege.
Especially we pray for all whose labour is increased at this season and for
whom the traffic of the marketplace drowns the song of the angels:
all who serve in busy shops, on crowded transport and in postal delivery,
that they may know your peace.

O Lord Jesus Christ, who was a refugee from your town and your country,
grant your mercy to those who have lost nationality and background,
especially such as have come to this country,
to the dependants at home of those who have escaped,
and to those who have failed to escape, and to all who suffer.
Keep our memories long, O God, and our hearts sensitive.

O Lord Jesus Christ, who for our sakes endured weakness and pain,
be with all who are ill, bedridden, fearful of their future health.
Raise to health those for whom health is appointed,
and enable them all to bear their afflictions in your faith.

O Lord Jesus Christ, who in love came down to earth,
assure of your love and of your forgiving mercy all who are burdened with
failure and guilt, and especially any who doubt whether they dare come to
your Holy Table.

O Lord Jesus Christ, who by your death vanquished death,
accept our praise for the victory you have won for all your people, and for the
memory of our friends, teachers, loved ones, who are now in your presence.

And to you, O Lord, as to the Father, and the Holy Spirit, be all honour and
glory, now and forever.

# CHRISTMAS

1.  Most blessed God, we worship and adore you.
    We come before you in hope and in expectation,
    for you have never failed or disappointed your people.
    You have ever kept tryst with them, have in love come forth to meet them.
    And when the time was ripe, you sent forth your Son: when your people's
    need is greatest, you ever stand before them in love and succour.
    And because you are unchangingly the same, waiting to show your glory
    anew to us in the face of Jesus Christ, therefore we wait upon you and adore
    your grace.

    God, who has taught us so much of yourself and revealed so much of your
    nature and purposes in Jesus Christ,
    we confess to you that our lives have too often been blind to your call and
    invitation, and that we have not shown the true image of yourself.

    From us, people might have learned that you were careless of them, when
    you love them with the love of Bethlehem and Calvary,
    that you have concern for some and not for others, when you care for them
    with unwearied favour,
    that you wait for us to make our approach to you, when you yourself came
    forth to seek and to save the lost.

    Forgive us, O God, for what we have failed to see and to understand, what
    we have failed to do and to be, and for all we have done amiss.

And give us grace at this season with wondering eyes to behold again our Saviour made human and born a child, for us and for our salvation, that we may fall before him and adore, and may rise up and follow him, who taught us to call you Father and to say Our Father . . .

2.   Eternal God, who has given to your church the word of this good news to
      proclaim to all the world,
      grant to your church such goodwill and concern,
      such love and such faith,
      that the message may be received as true,
      and may be believed and obeyed.
      To your people in every land,
      but especially where hardship and danger attend the confessing of your name,
      give joy and peace today,
      through Jesus Christ our Lord.

      O God who sent your Son to be the world's peace,
      we confess our part in the world's sin.
      Teach us, O God, from the beginning the way of peace,
      and guide the leaders of the nations to follow it,
      that your will may be done on earth.
      And wherever out of travail and strife many cry to you today,
      may the word of your love for every human being lead us anew to honour
      one another for Jesus' sake.

      For our own families and loved ones and friends we pray today,
      that children may rejoice,
      and that the opportunity for sharing with one another and with the needy
      may bring added joy.

      We remember those for whom today is shadowed by loss and hardship,
      by loneliness and ill health,
      and we commend to you those whose thoughts are with us,
      and whose needs are laid upon our hearts,
      that they may know comfort and joy at this season.

Especially we ask that the offerings we have made to you may be sanctified by you for the relief of need and for the succour of the destitute.

We praise you, O God, for those dear to ourselves who once shared in the joy of this day with us, but who now have entered into the joy unspeakable of your kingdom.

3.  Let us pray for the Church.
    O God, who gave to your holy angels glad tidings of great joy to those who watched and to those who slept,
    give to your church in these days such joy and such urgency in the proclamation of your gospel,
    that all your people themselves recognising in Jesus the promised redeemer,
    may so live and speak and work that the world may receive the word with joy, through the same Jesus Christ our Lord.

    Let us pray for the world which Christ came to save.

    O God, who so loved the world that you sent your only begotten Son for its salvation,
    we confess our part in the sin of all humanity by which your pleasant places have been made into a wilderness,
    your gifts have been perverted and misused,
    your children have been divided from one another by suspicion and hatred and ignorance.
    Hold steady before us the vision of a world of people and nations as people with one another because they have found their peace in you, and guide the leaders of the nations to yearn for and strive after the peace which is your will, through Jesus Christ our Lord.

    Let us pray for every agency that seeks to aid the needy and the helpless.

    We bless you, O God, for every agency concerned with bringing relief and comfort and hope to those who are in need.
    O God, you know how soon we weary in doing good work, and excuse ourselves because the needs are so great and the demands so many from doing what we ought to do and giving what we ought to give.

Prosper we pray all who serve their neighbours beyond the call of duty,
all who give to a point of sacrifice,
all who pray and weary not in their praying,
and give us a like compassion and diligence from the beginning of the year
even to its end, through Jesus Christ our Lord.

Let us pray for those whose Christmas is shadowed by loneliness, and
by loss, and who face the coming year with empty hearts, with weakened
bodies and spirits that have little of hope or joy in them.

O you who are able to succour your own in every time of travail,
who can give light to those who sit in darkness
and guide the feet of the troubled into the way of peace,
we earnestly commend to you all your sick ones, all your sad ones, all your
lonely ones, all your fearful ones.

4.  Almighty and eternal God,
    who calls your people to behold the majesty of your grace and the wonder
    of your love,
    to ponder the mystery of the incarnation,
    help us to understand the humility of our Lord Jesus Christ who laid aside
    his glory, and took upon himself the form of a servant,
    and the grace of our Lord Jesus Christ, that though he was rich, yet for our
    sakes he became poor, that we through his poverty might be rich;
    and the love of our Lord Jesus Christ who came not to be served but to
    serve, and to give his life as a ransom for many,
    and the perfect will of you, our Father, who was in Christ reconciling the
    world to yourself.
    And grant that we be not only hearers, but doers of the word, that it may
    bring forth in us fruit unto salvation.

5.  Come and let us walk in the light of the Lord.
    If we walk in the light, as he is in the light,
    we have fellowship with one another,
    and the blood of Jesus Christ, his Son, cleanses us from all sin.

Lord God, who has led us out of the darkness of the past night into the light
and promise of a new day and the promise of a new week, we worship you.
O God, who has given us a dayspring from on high, to visit and redeem
your people, we worship and adore you.
O God, who has given the light of your glory in the face of Jesus Christ,
we worship and adore you.

# LAST SUNDAY OF THE YEAR

1. Almighty God, who has given us one blessing above every blessing:
   life in Jesus Christ, justification by his death and rising again,
   peace with you through him,

   For this mercy which changes not from year to year,
   but which yet is ever new and ever wonderful, we bless you O Lord.

   We remember, O God, the other blessings that we have had from your hand
   in the past year as a congregation of your people in this place.
   The blessings of our common fellowship,
   your gifts to us from your word and through the sacraments.
   We thank you for all the prayers that you have answered,
   for lives that you have spared,
   for children safely brought into the world and by baptism received into the church,
   for those who have been joined in marriage,
   for all who have taken vows of loyalty to Christ and have been admitted to
   his table,
   for freedom from accident and danger to our children,
   for all that we have been able to do and to give and to learn,
   we thank you, O God.

   For your mercies to ourselves we thank you:
   for your goodness that has created us,
   your bounty that has sustained us,
   your fatherly discipline that has corrected us,
   your patience that has borne with us.

For every joyous experience and every precious memory that abides with us, we thank you,
for every chastening experience,
for every dark valley that you have yet led us through,
for every closed door that has yet opened,
for every time that you have shamed our fears or our doubts or our dismay, we thank you, O God.

Hear us as we bring the whole world into our prayers.

Build up, O God, your church and lead it by whatever way you have appointed for it.
Be near all servants of the church who labour in lonely or difficult places, especially those dear to ourselves.
Bestow your blessing upon this parish, its homes and schools; may peace and blessing be with them in the year to come.

We pray for this congregation, that we may do your work with joy and may not fall short in our responsibility to one another and to those around us.

We pray for the peace of the world; for the leaders of the nations, and for our own land and for the Queen and all the royal house. And for all the Queen's counsellors and all in authority over us that you will direct their counsels and endeavours, that this nation might be wisely governed and may be used towards the peace and unity of the world.

We pray for those whose year ends in sadness, and for the lonely and for the sick. Give them comfort and peace; enable them to lift up their hearts to the Lord, and to go forward with joy and with hope, knowing that their Lord is near.

Lord, above all worlds, we remember before you with thanksgiving those who have passed from this world into your own light and life, especially for those who have left us in the year that is past.

Give us grace as the years go by, to live in closer and closer communion with Jesus Christ.

2. O immortal Lord God, who inhabits eternity
   and has brought us to the close of another year,
   pardon all our transgressions in the past,
   and stay with us through all the days:
   Guard and direct the future as you have the past,
   that at the last we may finish our course with joy.

   Through Jesus Christ our Lord, who lives and reigns with you and the Holy
   Spirit, world without end.

   If we have rejoiced in fellowship with one another
   but have not found fellowship in you:
   If we have spoken and sung the name of our Lord
   and have given him no room in our hearts:
   If we have rejoiced in the gifts received from others,
   and have not coveted the best gifts, which are from you:
   forgive us.

   We bless you for every remembrance of our Saviour's coming,
   for every opportunity to remember and provide for our neighbour's need,
   for all good things that you have given us richly to enjoy, we bless you,
   but above all for the coming in flesh of your Son, born before all worlds,
   by whom the world was made, made human for us and for our salvation.

# LENT AND HOLY WEEK

1.  Jesus told his disciples, "If any want to become my followers, let them deny themselves and take up their cross and follow me." (Matthew 16:24)

Eternal God, who changes not in your mercy and love for your people,
in the name of Jesus Christ, who has brought to light your forgiving grace,
we offer worship – creatures to the Creator, children to the Father.
We bow before your majesty, we praise and magnify your name,
we wait upon your grace.
We look up to you who has yet looked upon us in love through your beloved
Son, our Saviour.

O you, who are of purer eyes than to behold iniquity, but who so regarded the sin of humankind as to send your Son to be made sin for us, we acknowledge our part in the sin of the world – our blindness of heart, our selfishness, our disobedience, our faithlessness.

We confess all the devious workings of our minds whereby we seek to assure ourselves of our own self-deception, all our excuses that we may not be seen by you in our poverty and our need.

Merciful Father, reveal to us ourselves, and set before our eyes the cross of our Saviour Christ, who is our hope and our life, who beyond all deserving has loved us, who while we were yet sinners died for us.

Father, we would seek in these days to enter into the mystery of your love and of your redemption. We would seek to look to Jesus, the author and finisher of faith.
We would desire to know him, and the power of his resurrection and the fellowship of his sufferings.

Come to us, O Lord, in the power of your Holy Spirit,
renew your covenant with us, assure us of your grace and strengthen us,
that we meet the toils and sufferings of our daily life with faith and patience;
and so strengthen us by your good Spirit that being delivered from the

snares and temptations by which we are constantly beset,
we may in all things be more than conquerors through him that loves us,
washes us from our sins in his own blood, even Jesus Christ, to whom with
you and the Holy Spirit be honour and glory, world without end.


2.   Eternal God, before we were born, you were alive.
Before time began, you were.
An infinity of ages and of universes are in your keeping.
And we here send out our little signals of prayer and awareness and concern,
little tendrils of love and appeal and desire,
feeling after you, hoping that we may find you.
And yet we believe, O our Father, that you are not infinitely remote from us,
that we are not indistinguishable grains of dust in your sight,
but men and women in the full tide of life,
and boys and girls whose names other people forget but whose names and
lives you know and care about.
That we are real people in your sight,
that you share our loneliness and our misgivings,
our happiness and our despair,
that you are acquainted with all our ways.
We know that we are stunted in many ways,
that we have not grown to our full stature and our full capacity.
We are dry bones and we need flesh and sap and spirit.

Give us help, O God, to derive strength from you in our worship,
that we may be renewed and invigorated.
Give us help, O God, to share our faith and our hope and our love more
with one another,
like living stones built into an enduring building.
Give us help, O God, to do more for other people than we do.
Give us help, O God, to live in the presence and power of Jesus Christ our
Lord every day, that his life may inform our lives,
his service be the purpose and meaning of all our living.
The Lord is from everlasting to everlasting.
The Lord is in this place.

3.  Father, we come from the common things of money and work, of home
    and garden, children and old people, to the mystery of bread and wine.
    The table is set, and in its whiteness it extends even to where we are, our
    elbows upon it, our hands resting upon it as we pray.

    Almighty God, give us oneness and expectancy, and hope and faith,
    that this be not ritual,
    conformity to a tradition handed down,
    but reality and confidence and newness of mind and of conviction.

    You shall have a song, as in the night when a holy feast is kept, and gladness
    of heart as when one sets out to the sound of the flute, to go to the mountain
    of the Lord, to the Rock of Israel.

    We think so much of ourselves,
    our successes, our failures, our needs, our importance.
    We see ourselves as unique, to excuse thereby the sins that so many before
    us for the same reasons have committed.
    We regard ourselves as special cases to explain why we should receive
    special consideration at your hands.
    But in our hearts we know that we are men and women,
    created by you and for your service,
    and we have been less than we should have been.
    We have made vows to Christ and we have betrayed him.
    We are thankful to have been brought to birth when we were, and not 2000
    years ago, or we would have forsaken Christ and fled, or with the others
    shouted "Crucify!",
    thankful that we did not grow to maturity in the 30s in Germany,
    in the 50s in China, when our faith would have been too openly put to the test.
    But even in our own day we have compromised too much, and confessed
    too little. O God, forgive what we confess now to one another in love,
    fuse us to those sitting beside us, whose elbows we hesitate to touch with
    our elbow, by the power of love and of a shared redemption and a shared
    joy, that in word and sacrament, our hearts may be warmed, and our life
    find its meaning.

4. O God, who created and sustains the world,
   we bow in worship before your glory and power.
   We bow before your love unmeasured,
   by which you have redeemed and blessed the world in Jesus Christ your Son.

   We offer praise to you, and to our King, Jesus Christ our Lord,
   who has suffered for us,
   being wounded by our transgressions and wounded for our iniquities,
   who for our sakes mounted the cross,
   enduring the last darkness of abandonment and the pains of death,
   that we might be delivered from pain and fear and death.

   We glorify his name, who reigns from the cross, having conquered every foe,
   who by his love,
   and his humiliation,
   and his sacrifice,
   has established his claim over our lives.
   While we were still sinners, Christ died for us.
   We who have sinned against all that we have learnt and known of your
   love and of your will for us, plead anew his righteousness to cover our
   unrighteousness, his obedience to atone for our disobedience,
   his conformity to your will to plead for our rebellion against your will.

   Saviour of the world, who by your cross and precious blood has redeemed
   us, save us and help us, we humbly ask you, O Lord.

   Look, Father, look upon his anointed face, and only on us as found in him.
   For between our sins and their punishment, we set the passion of your Son,
   our Lord.

   Renew in us this day, O Lord, the desire to follow in the footsteps of Christ.
   Grant to us that constrained by the love of Christ we may be drawn to him,
   and may accept our destiny as servants and fellow-workers with him who
   once died for us, and whose love is from eternity to eternity the same.

# EASTER

1.   "If in this life only we have hope in Christ, we are of all people most miserable: but now Christ is risen." (1 Corinthians 15:19)

O Lord our God, we give thanks to you for Easter day.
For the assurance that Jesus Christ is your Son,
and that he is the Saviour of the world,
and that all power is given to him.
For the conviction renewed within us that the meaning of our life is found in the cross and the empty tomb.
For the claim laid anew upon us that Christ is sovereign.
For the hope set before us that victory remains with love.

With the first disciples who learnt with wonder that the Lord was risen,
we would give glory to you.
With disciples through the ages who as Easter day has come have known that it was all true.
In fellowship with the millions throughout the world who keep this day with us.
In fellowship with the church in heaven,
those who have already entered into the fullness of the victory won this day,
we give you adoration and praise.
Almighty God who brought our Lord Jesus back from the dead,
grant us today with fresh eyes to see and with sincere hearts to believe,
and with all our souls to confess him our Lord and our God.

Forgive us, O God,
who have been so slow to believe, so slow to obey.
Forgive us, O God,
who have refused the comfort of him who has conquered death, and the daily help of him who has conquered sin.

Speak to our hearts the words that will declare forgiveness for sins past,
strengthen in testings yet to come,
and put hope in the days lying before us.

Lord Jesus, stand among us in your risen power,
and be known to us in your mercy and grace.

And to you, who with the Father everlasting and the Spirit of life now lives
and reigns forever, we will ascribe all glory on this day and for evermore.

2. O Lord our God, who has called us to newness of life by the resurrection of
your Son Jesus Christ from the dead,
that we should not be dead in trespasses and sins but should live in him,
we beseech you that the new life of Easter morning may come to us,
bringing us pardon and the sure hope of an endless life with you.
O God, we confess that we have walked in the dark places of the world,
in fear and in doubt,
that our lives and witness have not shown forth the living Christ.
We have not walked as those who are born again into newness of life.
We have been overwhelmed by the suffering and the injustices of the world
and before the mystery of death, and have not lifted up our eyes to behold
him who overcame sin and suffering and death itself, and who leads us in
the train of his victory.
We confess, O God, our unbelief, how we have followed you far off in fear
and trembling,
how unwilling to entrust ourselves to the keeping of the risen and
triumphant Lord, we have struggled on in our own helplessness, when all
the resources of the gospel were available to us through faith.

O Lord, have mercy upon us, and forgive us, and grant that being risen with
Christ we may ever seek those things which are above.

3. Christ our Passover is sacrificed for us: therefore let us keep the Feast.
Christ being raised from the dead dies no more,
death has no more power over him.
Thanks be to God who gives us the victory through our Lord Jesus Christ.

Praise be to you, O Father almighty, who delivered your Son to the death of the cross, and raised him up to newness of life, that we might live through him.
Praise be to you, our Lord Jesus Christ, delivered for our offences, raised again for our justification, who reigns in glory.
Praise be to you, O Holy Spirit of God, who bestows life upon the dead, who has shed abroad the love of Christ in our hearts, who can interpret to us his passion and his resurrection.
All praise and thanks, dominion and power, be unto you, O Holy and blessed Trinity, now and evermore.

Almighty God, who brought again from the dead our Lord Jesus, grant us with fresh eyes this day to see and sincere hearts to believe, and with all our souls to confess him our Lord and our God.
Forgive us, O God,
who so often live as those who have gone our own way, when a living Lord was at hand to lead and to guide.
Forgive us, O God,
who so often have struggled on in our own strength,
when all the resources of the Gospel were available to us through faith.
Forgive us that we have been cast down and dismayed by the changes and chances of the world, when our Saviour Christ has overcome the world.


4. Let us pray for the church.
O God, who calls your people to be witnesses to the resurrection,
purify and kindle your church in these days ,
and grant to her such joy and urgency in the proclamation of the Gospel,
that all your people, themselves abiding in Christ,
may so live and speak and labour that the world may receive their testimony
not as idle tales but as the very word of God.

God, who has promised your Son the uttermost parts of the earth for his possession,
we pray for those who from our midst have gone forth and will yet go forth bearing the word of life.
Hasten the day when all people shall know him as Saviour and worship him as Lord.

Let us pray for the world for whose salvation Christ died and rose again.
O God, who sent forth your Son to be the propitiation for our sins and not for ours only but for the sins of the whole world,
we confess our part in the sin of all humanity
whereby your pleasant places have been made a wilderness,
your gifts have been perverted and misused,
and your children divided from one another by suspicion and hatred and ignorance.
Hold steadfast before us the vision of a world of people and races and nations at peace with one another because they have found their peace in you.
We pray for this people, the Queen and her house, and the nations of the commonwealth, that the peace and righteousness which are your will may be manifest.

Let us pray for those who seek to celebrate this day under the shadow of loneliness and loss, and who face coming days with weakened bodies and with spirits that have little of hope or joy in them.
O God, who are able to succour your own in every time of travail,
who can give light to those who sit in darkness,
and breathe your peace upon the troubled,
we earnestly commend to you all your sick ones,
all your sad ones,
all your lonely ones,
all your fearful ones.
And especially those whom in the silence of our hearts we name before you.
As you have made us one people for worship and service and prayer, so hear now our prayers for one another.

# ASCENSION

1. O God, who dwells in glory and in splendour and in light unspeakable,
   we whom you have made offer our adoration to you.
   No one comes to you, except through Jesus Christ your Son.
   In his name we approach you.
   We have seen him,
   and thereby we know that we have seen you,
   and we are assured of your love for each one of your people,
   and have learned to call you Father.

   Risen, ascended and now among us, he calls us as his friends.
   Give your healing, O Christ, to us who require it.
   Give your strength to us who are weary.
   Give your comfort to us who are sad.
   Give your peace to us who are easily fretted and burdened by the cares of
   our lives.

   Renew your calling to us who have wandered from our call,
   and set upon the path again our feet that have lost the way.
   Knit us, O Christ, to one another, in responsibility and love.
   Knit us, O Christ, to you, in the bonds of trust and service.
   Renew in us the joy of the salvation that we have in you
   who taught us when we pray to say, Our Father . . .

# PENTECOST

1. We bless you, O God, and we worship you,
   because you are sovereign over your creation,
   because you have made the world,
   before all ages have appointed its redemption,
   and have ordained the day when time shall end and your majesty and your
   sovereign love shall be shown forth.

We bless you because we, creatures of a day,
who are easily cast down and dismayed by the changes and chances of the
world, are content that our destinies and the destinies of our children's
children are in the hands of such as you have shown yourself to be in
Jesus Christ our Lord.

Therefore we lay down before you our fears,
we lay down before you our burdens,
we lay down before you our weariness,
and from your word and from your worship we would draw again strength,
comfort, fortitude.

You, O Lord, will keep us in perfect peace whose minds are stayed on you;
because we trust in you.
In you we trust.
May your peace garrison our hearts that we may serve you without fear.

Father, we have cause to seek your forgiveness,
because in the work of your kingdom we have fallen short,
in the conduct of our daily work and business we have not earned your
commendation.
In the personal relationships of home and friendship we have not shown
the love and understanding that are commanded of us.
Father, forgive us, cleanse us, and if need be, reform and convert us.
Deepen our faith, our commitment to you, and our love for one another.


2. Lord, we wait quietly now to catch our breath before you,
   For life is hectic, and demands are many, and we run readily out of steam.
   We need the oxygen of your Spirit to enable us to breathe deeply and to
   work effectively.

   We bless you because the Spirit that once moved over the waters of creation
   is the same Spirit enlivening our worship, stirring our hearts, and moving
   us to offer our prayers and hymns of praise today.

It is by your Holy Spirit that all creation comes to pass and all renewal too.
By your Spirit in the beginning of days the world came to be.
And so order was imposed upon chaos and your purpose began to be fulfilled.
So human love began and human creativity,
and children were conceived and brought to birth, and family life developed;
and the fields were tilled and great cities were built,
and the wheels turned; and history took its shape,
by your Spirit.

By your Spirit human beings learnt of your will, and spoke and wrote of it.
By your spirit they recognised the Christ, and found the living Christ dwelling in them and going forth with them.

And in our day we need still your Spirit to brood over the chaos we have created,
to impregnate our weary and decayed spirits,
to invigorate and energise us, so that the world may find meaning and purpose and hope,
that love may be renewed, and community established.

Look in this month upon all that is dried and withered – and upon all that waits to break forth into new life.
Look upon your Church worldwide that awaits the winds of life to blow through it, driving us together, sweeping us forth.
We rejoice in all that we have seen of new life stirring, new hopes coming to birth, new vision taking shape.

Renew us in this our own land: help us to act together, to serve and believe together.
Grant that those who carry burdens of responsibility too heavy to be borne may find fresh wind to uplift and sustain them,
that new momentum may take us out into the communities of our land to do the continual work of mission, that special endeavours in these days may consolidate and rejuvenate the spirit of evangelism,
and that in these lengthening days of light and warmth we may be freshened and cleansed by that same spirit,
that we may be equipped to do the work to which the Church in every season and in every year is called, and may glorify Father, Son and Holy Spirit, one God blessed for ever.

3. O Lord Jesus Christ who sent from the Father the comforter, even the Spirit of truth: grant that your Spirit may enlighten our minds with the teaching of your truth, and sanctify our hearts with the power of your grace, so that ever abiding in you, we may be found steadfast in faith and holy in life, being conformed to your holy image, who are with the Father and the Holy Spirit ever one God, world without end.

4. We praise you O God, we give you thanks; we adore you, the giver of all good things.
We bless you for the manifold gifts of your love, and for the goodness and mercy that have followed us all our days.
We praise you for the unspeakable gift of Jesus Christ your Son our Saviour. Especially this day we magnify your name for the coming of the Holy Spirit, to take of the things of Christ and show them to his people, and to fulfill in them his work of grace. We bless you for the gifts you bestow through your Spirit, whereby you enable us to will and to do of your good pleasure. With thankful hearts give us obedient wills, and enable us to serve you faithfully all the days of our lives.

Almighty God who sent your Holy Spirit to abide with your church, to be its light and its comfort and its guide, gift the same gift to us, to help our infirmities and teach us to pray.
Look upon the neediness and poverty of your church we pray; gift us for the winds of life, that we may not be stifled by the graveclothes of our past life, but may know your grace for this and every day.
Bestow your enlivening grace upon the church in this land. Help us to spread abroad the word of life, till all peoples hear it in their own tongue. Further the work of the mission partners of the church, and of Bible societies and those who spread Christian literature.

Bless this parish, O God, and this congregation of your people; that the fire of the Holy Spirit may descend upon us, and the grace of Christ may be seen and known in every home.
Bless this land, the Queen and her ministers. Grant just government to us and to lands which are our neighbours, that liberty and peace may be sought and reverenced.

We recall before you all souls which are dried and parched and need the winds of life to blow through them.

There are many who are sick in body, and you can heal them, O Christ.

There are many who are sick in mind, and you can restore health and order.

There are many who are ailing in spirit and in soul, even unto death, and you can breathe upon the dry bones and the withered spirit and bring life.

To your mercy we commend them all, and as a believing fellowship of your church we now give ourselves in silent prayer for those and others whom we now name . . .

Jesus said "Those who believe in me, even though they die, will live, and everyone who lives and believes in me will never die". For these and all the promises of your grace we praise and glorify your holy name, Father, Son and Holy Spirit, one God, forever.

5.  Father God we believe that as a father pities his children, so the Lord pities us.
    That as a father provides for his children, cares for them,
    yearns and hopes and works for their wellbeing,
    so you our God yearn for us, provide for us, care about us.
    We put our hands in yours, Lord Jesus Christ, once young as we are,
    once human and oppressed by work as we are,
    tempted as we are, aware of human sufferings as we are,
    knowing our every experience from your experience,
    we put our hands in yours.

    Holy Spirit, unseen but always present,
    working in your world,
    seeking to work in us and through us,
    giving energy, and courage, and comfort,
    showing us the reality of Christ, and bringing him near to us,
    We confess our faith in you and our desire to know you.
    Before we speak further, we must speak of the things that have not been right in our lives, through our own choices and through our own refusal to do what we know to be right.
    As we think of them, remember them, confess them, are sorry for them, turn us from them, and give us forgiveness.
    Help our worship now and be with us through this day that we may enjoy it, and be glad in it for Jesus' sake.

# TRINITY

1. The Lord is near to all them that call upon him, to all that call upon him in truth. He will fulfill the desire of them that fear him. He also will hear their cry and will save them.

Almighty God, most blessed and most holy,
before the brightness of whose presence the angels veil their faces,
with lowly reverence and adoring love we acknowledge your infinite glory
and worship you, Father, Son and Holy Spirit, eternal Trinity.
Blessing and honour and glory and power be to our God forever and ever.

Almighty God, who is worthy to be served in every moment of our lives, and
of the disciplined loyalty and the loving devotion of our hearts,
we confess the self-indulgence and self-centredness that mark too much of
our lives,
the partial obedience,
the qualified love,
the failure to reach full Christian maturity.
We acknowledge these and much else, and ask for grace to be conformed to
the pattern you have marked out for our lives.
Give us today a new vision,
a new understanding of the needs of others,
a new compassion,
and a renewed dedication to the service of him who has shown us what life
can be and has given us a pattern of prayer in the words, Our Father . . .

2.  Eternal God, we bless you for all your goodness to us at this time,
    that we have been enabled to remember the death of Christ for us, and to
    receive again of his grace.
    Grant us to live as those who are not their own,
    but who know themselves to have been bought with a price,
    with the blood of Jesus Christ your Son our Lord.

    And now, Father, as you have made us one with your whole church in earth
    and heaven, and as we go from here to seek to take our part in the mission
    of the church, lift our eyes to behold the field in which you call us to work.

    You have taught us in Christ our dependence upon each other, and our
    responsibility for each other, so hear now our prayers which we pray in the
    name of Jesus Christ our Lord.

    We identify ourselves in your sight with all to whom we are sisters and brothers
    by our common humanity; in particular with those whose lives have been
    broken and ravaged by war, with the victims of human cruelty and injustice.

    Give us, O God, such width of vision, such love, that neither race nor colour,
    nationality nor creed may determine our reactions, but humanity and need.
    As we have received from the hands of Christ that were stretched out in love
    for the whole world, so teach us to give freely and gladly.

    We identify ourselves with all whom we live among and for whom we are
    responsible. In particular, we ask for strength to bear the burdens of the
    weak, to share the pains of the sick, and to commit them daily as we do now
    into your strong hands of mercy and love.

    We identify ourselves with the church unseen, with those who have gone
    before us in the way of discipleship, asking that we may so walk through life
    as those who know that they are seen by multitudes who care.

    We thank you for their love and prayers and example, and ask that our lives
    may be worthy of them, that with them we may be made perfect, and may
    join our thanksgivings with theirs through Jesus Christ our Lord, who lives
    and reigns and is worshipped and glorified, with you O Father, and the
    Holy Spirit, world without end.

# HARVEST

1.  Praise God from whom all blessings flow.
    Praise him all creatures here below.
    Praise him above ye heavenly host.
    Praise Father, Son and Holy Ghost.

    Almighty God, through whom we live and move and have our being,
    we give thanks for what we have eaten today,
    what we wear today,
    what we have sung today,
    the thoughts of thankfulness that fill our minds today.

    It was not of our choosing that we live where we life and how we live.
    It is not of our deserving that we are not impoverished and hungry and
    without hope in the world.
    It is not for our believing that we have heard of Christ and found our
    confidence and trust in our heavenly Father.
    Your mercies are so many and so great, far far more than we deserve.

    Have mercy upon our ingratitude, and help us with full hearts to give
    thanks, and by love and life to show our responsibility to others for the
    sake of him who though he was rich yet for our sakes became poor, that he
    might make many rich.

2.  Father God, we pray as members of the one world to which we belong, the
    one human family to which we belong.
    In order that we might rightly pray for them, we pray for ourselves;
    that we may always recall the hungry man at our shoulder,
    that we may not squander what you have entrusted to us as though it were
    our own,
    but that our stewardship may be real and our faithfulness may abide.
    Those things we therefore desire and are trying to bring about we commit
    to your greater power:

the feeding of the hungry,
the clothing of the needy,
the feeding of impoverished human minds.

We pray that honour may be seen to belong to those who serve their neighbour, that men and women of humility may be seen to be the greatest of all in the kingdom.

We pray for the poor and despised among the nations of the earth, and even within our society.
We glorify you for those whose life is given to the service of them.
We pray for those we know whose lives have been impoverished by the death of some near to them.

# ALL SAINTS

"Blessed are the pure in heart, for they will see God. Blessed are those who are persecuted for righteousness' sake, for theirs is the kingdom of heaven." (Matthew 5:8, 10)

Almighty and everlasting God,
who has been in all ages the refuge and strength of your people;
one generation shall praise your works to another, and shall declare your mighty acts.
We who follow where many have gone before would worship and adore you, declaring your faithfulness and showing forth your praise.

O King of saints, who has manifested your wonderful love and power in the lives and deaths of your servants of old,
grant that we like them may have grace to glorify you,
loving you whom they have loved,
and finding the peace they have found,
and may come to dwell with them and with you for ever, in the gladness of your glorious presence, through Jesus Christ our Lord, who taught us to pray saying, Our Father . . .

# REMEMBRANCE

1. Remember Jesus Christ, risen from the dead.

   Bless the Lord, O my soul, and forget not all his benefits.

   O Lord, we who have received so much that we have not earned and have not deserved, with gratitude wait upon you.

   In thankfulness for life itself; that precious thing which has been granted to us, and spared to us thus far.

   For freedom, which men and women of old cherished and defended, and which women and men of our own day have sustained at great cost.

   With penitence, for we have been heedless and ungrateful, we come.

   With gratitude, for the Lord has done great things for us, of which we are glad, we come.

   With recollection, for we would remember our heritage and would seek to be worthy of it, we come.

   With commitment, that we may be strengthened to hand on what we have received, we come.

   In humble remembrance of those who went before us,

   In acknowledgement of our God who created us, and who gave once his Son for the life and wholeness of us all,

   In affirmation that we are not our own, for we are bought with a price, we make our worship to you, our God.

   And to pray for this nation of ours, the Queen and her house, for the institution of parliament and those who serve therein,

for armed forces of the crown,
those who seek to create justice for our people and to preserve order among
them, and to create prosperity for them,
for the churches in their mission,
for people of peace and of goodwill.

For the world's peace, and the world's salvation and the triumph of the
Kingdom, for all this we pray.


2. Almighty and eternal God, our refuge and our peace who in love gave your
own Son our Saviour even unto death that we might live through him, we
bless and worship you.

Everlasting Father, humbly and thankfully we remember before you those
men and women who in two world wars and since, gave all that they had,
even life itself, in defence of their homes and liberties, by whose death we
live, of whose sacrifice we are not worthy.

They shall grow not old as we that are left grow old. Age shall not weary
them, nor the years condemn.
At the going down of the sun and in the morning:
We. Will. Remember. Them.

Keep alive within our hearts, O God, the memory of the debt we owe.
Let their devotion ever be an example to us that we being faithful unto death
may at last receive the crown of life, through Jesus Christ our Lord.

3.  Almighty God, who is our refuge and our strength,
    we humble ourselves in your presence,
    and as we make solemn remembrance before you this day of the great
    things that have been done for us,
    we earnestly seek your mercy and your grace.

    We are not worthy, O God, of these things –
    we are not worthy of your great and redeeming sacrifice of your Son Jesus
    Christ for us.
    We have been forgetful of him, and of the vows which in time of trouble
    our lips have spoken.

    O Saviour of the world, who by your cross and precious blood has redeemed us,
      save us and help us, we beseech you, O God.
    Almighty God, who is King over all, and who has brought us to this day,
    we thank you for your goodness and gracious providence that guided and
    sustained this people in days of war,
    for grace that upheld us in days of peril and sorrow,
    and for our final deliverance.
    We cried out to you, and you heard us.
    Grant that, being mindful of your great goodness and of the undeniable
    claim that you have established over us,
    we may yield ourselves in new and penitent obedience to your will,
    and live as those who are not their own, but are bought with a price.

    Our help is in the name of the Lord, who made heaven and earth. I will say
    of the Lord; he is my refuge and my fortress, in him will I trust.
    Jesus said, "No one has greater love than this, to lay down one's life for
    one's friends."

# BAPTISM

1. O God, our Father and the Father of our children,
   we bless you for this sacrament and for the promise attached to it.
   As with humble faith, and assured of your love, we approach the font,
   look mercifully upon us, and ratify in heaven that which we do upon earth.
   O Blessed Saviour, who took little children into your arms and blessed them,
   take ＿＿＿ we beseech you and seal *her/him* for your own,
   who lives and reigns with the Father and the Holy Spirit, one God.

2. Eternal God, in whose nature we understand love and sacrifice and compassion,
   we thank you for your love for ＿＿＿ now received into the fold of your church,
   and we beseech your blessing upon *her/him* in body and in spirit, though
   the days of childhood and youth, that *s/he* may in happiness and goodness
   grow.
   Bestow your blessing upon the home within which you have set *her/him*,
   and upon your servants in this new responsibility you have laid upon them.
   And give grace to us all, whom you have made one family in Christ, bearing
   one another's burdens and sharing one another's joys, to care for one
   another, and to establish in this place a fellowship of service and of love.

3. Lord God, we thank you for your gift of life bestowed upon this baby, for
   your gift of health bestowed upon *his/her* mother, and for your gift of
   responsibility bestowed upon *his/her* parents and upon this congregation.
   We ask that as you have blessed them at this time, you will lead them on
   into fuller blessing.
   May this baby become a healthy child, and a *(wo)man* of grace and of that
   beauty that comes from faith and inner tranquility. May *his/her* life serve
   Christ and his Kingdom.
   Sanctify *his/her* home, that your kindness to *him/her* at this time may
   produce deepened joy and faith; that peace may dwell there, and love.
   And as we have all been baptized into one body, make the body of Christ in
   this place a unity in which every member will find its place, and serve with joy.

4. O God, the Father of the Lord Jesus Christ, and in him of all who believe and of their children, we thank you for your command that we have fulfilled, and your grace that you have promised and we have claimed.
We seek your grace upon ____ and upon *his/her* home and parents; that they all may be protected and guarded by you, and that you will fulfill in *him/her* what you have this day begun.

Give us grace, O God, to minister to *him/her* as a congregation in your name, and grant that wherever *s/he* may be in future days, the presence of Jesus Christ and the living community of his church may be the environment of *his/her* life as *s/he* grows to the fullness of Christian maturity.
Grant to *him/her* in childhood, adulthood, age and even until death to abide faithful to you who abides ever faithful, to whom be the glory now and forever.

5. God appeared on earth like this. And little children are dear to him.
He called them to himself and laid his hands upon them and blessed them. And in baptism he takes them for his own, that not as children only, but as grown men and women they may serve him in the family of the church. But at first, he entrusts to parents who love their children the responsibility of their Christian upbringing. So let us stand while the vows are taken:

O God, we bless you for parenthood and for infancy, alike sanctified by Bethlehem.
For the wonder of every infant life begun, the promise of it and the hope.
Look upon this little one, fulfill your great and good purpose in *him/her*, help *his/her* parents in the charge of this holy thing committed to them; make *her/him* strong in the Lord and a blessing to many.

# COMMUNION

1. The Lord said, "Now therefore, if you obey my voice and keep my covenant, you shall be my treasured possession out of all the peoples. Indeed, the whole earth is mine, but you shall be for me a priestly kingdom and a holy nation". (Exodus 19:5-6a)

Lord, the whole earth is yours, the beauty of it, the mystery of it. And we have been called into covenant with you, by your love shown to us in Jesus Christ.

We give thanks for all we have experienced of your world today.
We give thanks for all that we have today experienced of your mercy,
all that has come to us through human relationships and friendship,
and above all for all that we have seen and heard and tasted and handled of the word of life.

For faith renewed that Jesus Christ is Lord,
for every glimpse of reality, we give thanks.

Forgive us for all in which even today
our vision has been blurred and unfocused,
in which we have been hard of hearing,
in which we have side-stepped decisions,
in which we have turned aside from the way that we knew we were to take.

Set our feet upon the way,
give all of us a new beginning,
and a new momentum,
a new desire and readiness to follow Jesus Christ wherever he may lead,
and this for his sake.

2. God does not go back upon his gift or his call.
   The blessing of the Lord makes rich, and he adds no sorrow with it.
   Bless the Lord, O my soul, and forget not all his benefits.

Today, O God, we have had fellowship with one another,
in worshipping together, and so we bless you.

Today, O God, we have sung psalms and hymns of praise and of adoration,
with whatever voice you have given us,
and so we bless you.

Today, O God, we have heard your word read, have heard repeated the very
words that Jesus used,
and so we bless you.

Today, O God, we have pondered on the mystery of Christ's incarnate life,
his identification with us human beings, so that though we might fail to
recognise him, he might be our Saviour indeed,
and so we bless you.

Today, O God, we have stood before the cross, and remembered your Son's
body broken and his blood spilt, and all this for our sakes,
and so we bless you.

Today, O God, we have entered into communion with him, have renewed
our vows of loyalty, have offered ourselves our souls and bodies to be a
reasonable holy and living sacrifice, and you have heard our vows and
received our offering,
and so we bless you.

Today, O God, we have known ourselves to be sent out to live for Jesus
Christ and for no other. Today we have recalled our calling as Christians, as
Christ's men and Christ's women. Ransomed, healed, restored, forgiven –
who like me his praise should sing.

And so we praise and bless you.

# WEDDING PRAYERS

1.  Father, this is a family occasion for us. People who don't all know each other, but our thoughts, our affection, our lives, our goodwill focusing upon one or another, or upon both of the people whose voices will shortly be heard by the rest of us.

    We have dressed up specially for today to honour this occasion, and to show that it is important to us all.
    As families, we have come to celebrate this high moment in the histories of both families, in the intensity of our desire that _____ and _____ should find true fulfillment in their future living, should find that strange and vulnerable thing which is happiness, which comes only to those who don't seek it too hard for themselves. That they may cherish and honour the traditions from which each of them has come, and be enriched as these traditions now converge, that their lives may flourish and grow in a long span of years to come. These things as families we ask for.

    And the rest of us have come to share the pride of the families because _____ and _____ are our friends, and we too want to see this day as the high point of their lives thus far, to surround them with the warmth of our affection for them, to claim for them all that we believe marriage should offer.

    And because we are none of us adequate for these things, we entrust their relationship into your hands, as we also commit our own lives and relationships, grateful some of us for what we have known and enjoyed, seeking forgiveness where we ourselves have fallen short, and asking blessing on the days before us, through Jesus Christ our Lord.

2. For many, many things we give thanks.

   For the perfection of this day, in its light and its beauty.

   For the deep happiness of this day, for us gathered here, in its hope and its promise.

   O God, who gives your people life and love,

   purpose and fulfilment,

   whose will is for the happiness and peace of your people,

   we thank you for your purpose made visible through the changes and chances of our earthly life,

   for every human blessing,

   every dim aspiration,

   and on this day for marriage, the seal and assurance of your great gift which is love.

   Look upon us in what we say and seek and resolve.

   Enable your servants that the vows they take they may take seriously in your sight, and have grace to keep with joy all their days.

   We give thanks, O Lord, for much goodness bestowed upon us all.

   We commend to you your servants _____ and _____, and all who with them most share in the happiness of this day.

   Bless this new home established, this new household of your people.

# FUNERAL PRAYERS

1.  Eternal God, Father of us all, we offer thanks for many things, but especially
    today for family life and what it has meant in the experience of many of us,
    for those who have sustained it and given it meaning,
    for all the challenges and tensions and disciplines of family life,
    and its sacrifices,
    all of love that has come to us thereby, and of mutual support,
    and those in whom we have seen the costliness of it and the rewards of it.
    And so today for _____ we give thanks.

    We offer thanks for the disciplines of daily lives and of daily work,
    for those whose commitment and loyalty to that, and whose skill and
    dedication and responsibility and particular gifts of discrimination and
    sensitivity have been used to the full.
    And so too today for _____ we give thanks.

    We offer thanks for the width of human experience,
    for all the many-faceted glimpses of human life that we have shared with
    others who knew more than we did,
    who enlarged our own dimension as they shared with us what they had
    seen and found.


2.  Eternal God, we whose lives are short look to you who holds us in life,
    we whose knowledge is partial look to you, with whom is wisdom and who
    does all things well,
    we who are easily dismayed by the changes and chances of our mortal life
    would lean upon you, who do not change, and whose love and compassion
    were shown forever in your Son, Jesus Christ.
    We bless you for his life, which is the pattern of all good life,
    for his death, which he endured for our sakes,
    for his rising again, whereby he has drawn the sting of death forever, and
    opened a way of life into your eternal presence.

As Christian men and women,
we bless you for all the rich inheritance that we have in him,
the strength that is made perfect in our weakness,
the hope that no-one can take from us,
the love that will not let us go,
the peace that the world cannot give nor take away.

And so too today for _____ we give thanks.

We offer thanks for friendship,
for those who shared so much with us, without whom our lives would have
been impoverished and less colourful and less fulfilled,
those whose wisdom and freshness of thought and vitality of spirit, whose
profound values undergirding their living, gave a measure of direction to
our own living that we would not otherwise have known.
And so too today for _____ we give thanks.

We give thanks for all the happy memories that will abide in cheerful
reminiscence when the sadness of this day has passed,
and the faith that sustained _____ into the fullness of which s/he has now
come,
and that now s/he sees and understands those things which are yet beyond
our understanding, who do not understand the mystery of our coming or
of our going hence.

Guide and sustain us through the days of our pilgrimage, whether they be
long or short, and bring us too at the last through the merits of Christ to
the Father's house,
that we too may hear the words, "well done, good and faithful servant, enter
thou into the joy of the Lord",
and that we too, in the company again of those whom we love and for a time
have lost may understand the mystery and may behold the vision glorious,
through Jesus Christ, our Lord.

— SERMONS —

# A DAY OF THANKSGIVING

In the Gospel according to John, chapter 4, verse 35, Jesus' words: "I tell you, take a good look at the fields." Of course he was speaking to people for whom the fields were the environment of their lives. In other words, they lived in the middle of them and at the same time they probably never really looked at them at all. And certainly, when they were hanging on the words of Christ, the last thing they'd think of doing was looking at where life was for them and would be as soon as they stopped listening.

We live in a world where we hear so much about many things. You know what a sermon's going to be about and harvest thanksgiving these days is going to be clobbering you about Christian Aid, and guilt, and our good fortune and other people's bad fortune, to make you feel totally miserable. However you began the service, singing well, you'll end up feeling guilty and feeling you have to do something about it, but not necessarily enjoying doing it. I don't know if that is how it ought to be. I think it should be harvest thanksgiving above all things, not just "here's tae us, wha's like us," or "I thank thee Lord that I am not as other men are." But realising the infinite goodness and graciousness of God to all humankind.

The news we hear is always of the suffering and the starving. The thing that the Third World and those who are sensitive to the needs of the Third World greatly resent is when the Third World is presented always in terms of need, of large-eyed, hollow-faced children, of people in destitution. The best of the aid organisations have determined, only quite recently, that they're not going to do that any more. It's no ultimate help to present the Third World as simply requiring the aid of other people instead of being in itself often sufficient, adequate, full of confident people, of people who need the encouragement and the help at particular areas in order to be all that they ought to be.

News is a curious thing, what we read, what we fail to read, what we're told, what we fail to be told. The flyer for the Evening News on Friday, on the billboards – the day when historic decisions and speeches were being made by the Prime

Minister and others – was "Misery for Mum as slugs invade". I'm not sure who Mum was and I'm not sure why. I'm sure it was very miserable indeed, but this was the main thing that the News obviously wanted to sell its newspapers by. I recall the Daily Record a couple of weeks ago where the enormous headlines on the front page were: "Grandad's coffin was set on fire". Now these may be important things, probably important to Grandad, and certainly important to his family, but sometimes the news that is presented to us is of such a kind that we realise we're being shielded from what we can't bear to look at and yet from what we ought to know as well.

Here's a news item from the 1990s that you won't remember. It's to do with what used to be Yugoslavia, and it is quite simply that the leader of the Serbian Orthodox church, the patriarch there, and the Catholic Archbishop of Zagreb issued a joint appeal to the Catholic and Orthodox congregations in the former Yugoslavia and to the international community. What they were doing essentially was castigating their own people. "We're requesting that all hostilities, bloodshed and destruction, blasphemous and mindless destruction of both Christian and Moslem sanctuaries be immediately and unconditionally halted and that the warring sides urgently begin direct negotiations. We unanimously condemn all crimes and dissociate ourselves from all criminals, irrespective of their nation or army, and irrespective of which church or religion they say they belong to" and so on. The leader of the Moslem community in Bosnia was unable to leave Sarajevo in order to attend the meeting where the leader of the Roman Catholic and the Serbian Orthodox churches met to make this declaration, but they knew that he too was of one mind in this.

The spiritual leaders of the sections of former Yugoslavia were shown to be absolutely of one mind. But this kind of thing doesn't get the headlines because, in its own way, it's good news. It talks of reconciliation and concern, just as in Northern Ireland today we don't hear about the Roman Catholic bishop and the Presbyterian minister going together to the homes of Catholics and Protestants where some act of terrorism or murder has taken place – but this happens and it happens every week. But we don't hear these things because they are good news.

Today, let's concentrate on the good news then. Today, let us remember the element of thanksgiving that's involved in what we read or ought to read, what we reflect upon or ought to reflect upon. Now, we have not ploughed the fields or scattered good seed on the land – at least I haven't. But we've not been hungry, nor our children. We've survived thus long. Over half a century after the last bomb fell on the United Kingdom there have been no war-time bombs since. Over half a century after the last nuclear device was exploded in war and wilfully, there has been no other nuclear device thus exploded, miraculously. I know we're often led to feel that as long as one child is hungry in the world, we've no right to do other than mourn but our instinct tells us that that is not right. Jesus said, not in cynicism as it might at first seem but with realism, that there always will be the poor. And yet we laugh and yet we sing and we rejoice in thankfulness at the undeserving prosperity and benefits that so many have – that we have.

If we are aware of certain facts that are not immediately obvious to us, they are so obviously good news that we don't reflect upon them. That we have a system of parliamentary democracy. That we have a judicature and a law keeping force that are honourable, and act, in the main, with equity. That corruption and baksheesh and dash, whatever you call it, is part of our national life, for all people are human beings, but so much less than in many countries, so that the more we see of any other nation the more thankful we may be that we live where we do and as we do. That ought not to be complacency or smugness or heedlessness but quite simply thankfulness that we are as we are. The fact that we have an inherited faith and a church that, for all its failings, people are free to admit to membership of. Count your blessings. Name them one by one. Not your misfortunes. Not your anxieties but your blessings. And supremely today, and most primitively, that starvation and lack of food, pollution of water supply or drying up of water supply have not been our experience. This is a day of thanksgiving.

Of course, not the flip side of that but the reasonable consequence of that is that it also must be a day of concern for other people. The awareness of a world that we can do little for, but can do something for. It's a day for being disturbed and for being aware. A Christian has a right to be worried. A Christian has a right to have sleepless nights, but not because of himself or his own situation, but because people are hungry and in hazard of life and of health and because of the rampant injustice in the world. I think it is children that, before all else, we're aware of. We, whose children are mostly very fit and for whom provision of every kind can be made.

The Old Testament and the New Testament seem both to suggest that concern about these matters is not just derived from religion but is itself religion. Amos made it clear that for him the service of God was to right the injustices of society. He would question dubious business methods, as they were in his day, and presumably he would have questioned those in our day. To take just one example, great firms still transfer their manufacturing plants from the developed western world, with its concern for working conditions and safety standards and so on, to Taiwan or South Korea or Mexico where labour can be paid less and where organised resistance to bad conditions is so much less. Amos would have noted that and marked it. In the New Testament, such concern is not a consequence of Christian faith, it is itself Christian faith. It's not the totality of it but it's a fundamental constituent of it. True religion and undefiled, said the writer James, is to take care of the orphans and the widows in their suffering. And Jesus said that serving God did not lead people to care for the sick and the imprisoned, but that serving God was doing these things. The hungry of the world stand as God's judgement upon those who consume heedlessly and unthankfully.

The hungry of the world are an opportunity given by God. They are a criterion by which our society, not just will be judged on the last day, but is constantly under the judgement of God.

This is a day of thanksgiving, it's a day of concern and I suppose it has to be said that it is a day of action. And action is always more than worship. We talk about 'service' to represent this hour of prayer and reading and talking and singing. But Christian service perhaps is more than that. And this is not an alternative for the other.

I remember once, in the United States, meeting a lady from a church in Houston, what nowadays would be called a mega-church, one of the great churches with an enormous financial programme and great generosity and much else. She was not long back from a tour with her church choir over the great part of Europe, singing in cathedrals and in Britain too. She'd enjoyed it, though she and they had been together before. But she was disappointed because they had hoped to go to Brazil. The branch of the church she belonged to had particular connections with Brazil and had sent many, many missionaries there and so they'd written in good time saying they'd like to tour, please, with a choir of a hundred voices, being put up in the homes of the people. The local people had replied saying they would have liked to have heard the choir but they would find difficulty in putting up and feeding those numbers. But if they could maybe send a party of twelve, and it didn't matter if they couldn't sing much, but if they could include people good at mending leaking roofs, it would be a great help. And so the choir had toured Europe again once more.

Action means, I suppose, not just singing, however well we sing. It means influencing government policy. It means writing wearisome letters to many people. It means doing what Amnesty does month by month based in our church hall. It means signing letters to an over-worked and over-burdened Prime Minister. It means tackling the consciences that already are pricked but need to be ever and again pricked, especially our own consciences, so that we don't get charity fatigue, so that we don't weary in well thinking and well doing. To sing will never again be enough. To pray will be very important. To remember constantly will be imperative. And to make some kind of sacrifice, spending on this instead of spending on that. Harvest thanks, thanksgiving. Yes, of course, giving.

"Now abide," said Paul "Faith, hope and love, and the greatest of these is love." Perhaps our harvest thanksgiving will be a sign of that greatest thing of all which is Christian love, a sign of the love of God to us in Jesus Christ. Enjoy your thanksgiving day today. And those of you who come from the United States, enjoy your thanksgiving day when it comes too.

# A VERY ORDINARY SERVICE

"I'm certain that nothing can separate us from His love. Neither death nor life. Neither angel or other heavenly rulers or powers. Neither the present nor the future. Neither the world above, nor the world below. There is nothing in all creation that will ever be able to separate us from the love of God, which is ours through Christ Jesus our Lord." (Romans 8: 38 )

This is a very ordinary service today. In no way out of the ordinary, it's pure routine. I know that people in the front pews would, just possibly, want to dispute that. After all, some of them are there because of a particular, unrepeatable, event in the life of either themselves or of someone very close and dear to them. And there are people here today whose children have been introduced for the first time to the delights and rigours of Sunday School and who are listening with half an ear to their enjoying it, or otherwise, next door. And there may also be people here in consequence of the tragic loss of someone whose name has already been mentioned, perhaps by everyone of us in our prayers. But I would still say it is not an exceptional Sunday, or an exceptional service. It's just any old Sunday and the most natural thing in the world. And I say that though I'm aware that every Sunday someone or other, unknown to me and unknown probably to most of us, may be in this place seeking to do a deliberate U-turn in the midst of the highway of life. Someone or other may be in church for the first time for a decade, or giving the church one more chance to work upon his or her life, to bring conviction and to make a difference. It can be a climactic day in the life of one person or more than one. But that is surely part of the expectation of every act of worship. So what, apart from that, is normal about this service?

Well, firstly this: that worship itself, it seems to me, is a terribly normal activity. I believe there is an instinct to worship in every person. In our society, it's only a minority who translate it into the standard convention of going to church and engaging in this particular activity. In many societies today, as in our society for generations past, the sheer grind of poverty and hardship and hopelessness almost extinguishes it and it becomes more of an inner yearning. A lot of the mission hymns of a century ago reflect that, about the sweet by and by and the hopes one has, one day, of attaining bliss. Or you can secularise it in songs like "All I want is a nice arm chair, wouldn't it be loverly". And that in a sense is a kind of substitute for what we are calling worship. It's transmuted into the instinct of mother love, parental love. It can be transmuted into the passionately held belief in our Western world that we all have a right to happiness, though that doesn't come in the creed of any of the standard religions. It can find its substitute expression in nationalism, or in football fanaticism, or beliefs based on the direction that science seems still to be pointing us towards, in idolatries of various kinds, in hopes that people don't dare to articulate even to themselves. I think we might be hard put to explain rationally the form that our own religious expression takes – this fixed activity within an apparently statutory period of one hour. For us, worship is in the form that our culture requires of us but, even in our non-church-going society, I believe, the instinct is to find a satisfying form of worship and that instinct is not far below the surface. It may reduce itself to watching somebody on television on a Sunday evening.

Now, this that we do is not bizarre or unlikely, it's part of humanity's awareness of a measure of aspiration, of inadequacy and of hope, of moving towards something finer and nobler than we've known, and a dissatisfaction at where we stand as yet. Where we say, "Is this all that there is, this life that we know," and something within us says, "There is more than this," and some of us dare to use tried formulas to express it. And because the formula has been satisfying to us, more or less, we repeat it over and over again and are at home in it. We call it "going to church", we call it "worship".

There's something more that's terribly normal about this particular service, and that is the natural instinct to give our children the chance to discover what may be in store for them. To focus our pride in our children, our acceptance of responsibility for them, our recognition that there is something still miraculous about birth and about the creation of life, and act of human procreation that transmits genetic traits that are unique and recognisable. And so we say, some of us, that this is the setting of our offspring into the culture that we have inherited. It involves our responsibility, our sharing in this progress of maturity, of growth in understanding that we want for our children.

I read of the Church of England vicar in Liverpool to whose door there came a lady carrying a baby, and she said, "I would very much like to have my baby baptised. Could you possibly do it now while I go and do my shopping?" Well I'm not sure that that's all that far down the road from offloading one's child at the Church Hall door on a Sunday morning and picking it up on the way back from Sainsbury's half an hour later. It's a matter of responsibility: we're not handing it over – we're accepting it, not from the midwife or the surgeon or anybody else, we're accepting it now from God. And at the same time claiming from him the help to do what we want above all things to do: to enable our children to achieve what, or far more than what, we ourselves have achieved in fullness of life, in understanding of the mystery and wonder of the Godhead.

There's another natural thing today that makes the service very ordinary, and that is the acceptance presently by the congregation that some people are at a stage of certainty, or at least of diminished uncertainty, at which they want to say publicly on whose side they are. Again they are a minority. And that's maybe because no referendum is held on the issue of Christian commitment. The numbers of young people in their late teens making a deliberate 'No' vote, if pressed, might be far less than the number who would find it possible and necessary to say 'Yes', but we don't press this one way or the other. The act of the church's admission on confession of faith is a very moving thing often for those engaged in it and for those observing it, but it's not a dramatic U-turn for most of those who have passed through the process of Christian nurture, who've been surrounded by love, who've been given an example, however understated, however low-key, and who have found that the church is an environment which is not hostile or threatening or alienating but reassuring. They have found that, in fact, it is home.

We do no service to anyone if we say that to become a communicant is a drastically important plunge, or leap of faith, a new beginning, a changing of values and allegiance. It may be so in a pagan environment. It ought not to be so in a living Christian community. I would like to think that the three people who have taken this short course in preparation for going off to their studies elsewhere, who take their vows today, can do so without, as it were, breaking sweat. It is maybe not complimentary to them to have it put that way. But I hope that they recognise that this is a stage. "One more step along the world I go." One more staging post. One more camp site on the journey of pilgrimage that leads at the end to the promised land.

I seem to remember telling you, maybe more than once before, of the first camp that I ever went to as a school boy in Edinburgh. It was one of those very highly organised things for school boys and, for most of us – we were young – it was our first experience of camping under canvas, a great adventure. The thing was slightly diminished by the fact that the tents had all been pre-set before we arrived there and to be on the safe side they'd all been set out inside an enormous marquee. Now, there's a sense in which this dramatic staging, of going one stage on, one after the other within Christian faith, in fact is all done under the encompassing umbrella of the love of God. It isn't stepping out from the unknown. It isn't stepping into the unknown. It's rejoicing in the warmth of conviction that the God who has taken us thus far is going to take us another step yet. *The Scotsman* many years ago had an article on its sports pages which I cherish. It was about local athletics. It said that Edinburgh Southern Harriers were going ahead "by leaps and bounds". And so harriers should. Now that may be another experience, there are times when we go ahead by leaps and bounds, but I don't think that this is necessarily the case for those who take vows at this time, not for these particular people at least. This is simply a normal and natural event that is happening.

Each stage, baptism, worship, admission and even that something else that has to be said, the something else that is perhaps less than natural and inevitable about this service. The last week has faced people, many of us know, with the shattering break in their lives which is created by the death of somebody they love. There's nothing painless, there's nothing smooth about that experience. It changes everything – sometimes into bleakness and desolation. Sometimes there's an underlying sense of total thanksgiving and even of relief. But those who are so afflicted need more than anything to be comforted with a balm of understanding love and prayerful support. This is the hardest when death comes untimely and dramatically in the fullness of youthful promise, with so much unfulfilled. To say anything then to one another is very hard. And what I say now perhaps can't be taken as applying in those circumstances, although in later years there may be an understanding of this. But in most cases death is not to be seen by Christian people as an obscenity or irrationality, as any kind of denial of all that life is about, a blow in the face from a loving providence. It's far rather a stage in the life of us all. A fairly dramatic exit and entry into another setting, leaving grief and dismay for those who cannot share in that moment, though one day they too will experience it. After all, to be for ever with the Lord is the aim and the desire of Christian people throughout the course of this life. To this end we baptise. To this end we confirm the desire and reaffirm this conviction by confirming those who have been baptised. And the final resolution and confirmation that it is so is, we believe, in this event of death itself. A last enemy indeed and one day to be obliterated from human experience, but meantime, like every disease, every hardship, every circumstance, a situation in which the presence and power of God are yet to be looked for and experienced.

Death comes at the end to us all. If the experience is tragically and unnaturally foreshortened then the shock is grievous, but yet the process has been fulfilled by whatever mischance. For what we call life and what we call death are quite close to each other. To look them both in the face and to see Christ as present in each is so near the heart of Christian faith that it becomes for most Sundays to us also part of the normal act of worship. Every day brings news of terrible things. Every day gives us opportunity for assuaging pain, hunger and need. Every day is a day that the Lord has made. We accept it from his hand with all the unpredictabilities about it, with all the human joys and affirmations and tragedies about it and our worship gathers it all up and sends us out able to face, to conquer, to rejoice and to say: "This is one more week, one more day that the Lord has made and we will rejoice, be glad and achieve in it."

# ALL SAINTS DAY:
## THE WIDE FOCUSED LENS

"And I heard every creature in Heaven and Earth in the world below and in the sea, all living beings in the universe, and they were singing to him who sits on the throne and to the lamb, be praise and honour glory and might for ever and ever." (Revelation 5: 13)

A lifetime ago, a great film maker called Lewis Milestone made a film of a great book, a classic, *All Quiet on the Western Front.* Long before the days of wide screen, he represented something of the sheer scale of the tragedy and the waste and the horror of what, at that time, was the greatest war the world had ever seen. A generation later he was commissioned to direct another film about a still greater war, what we call World War II. But in this case he did not fill the screen with masses of figures stumbling and falling. Instead, he concentrated only upon one platoon and indeed, I think, upon one section of a platoon. An American infantry platoon in sun-baked Italy after, I think, the Salerno landing, which felt itself, as I suspect so many small infantry units could in war time, totally isolated, totally cut off from its friends, totally unaware of even where the enemy were, in what seemed to an empty landscape. For them, their war was quite simply this hedgerow, that sunken road, that field beyond and that silent farmhouse which was their objective. The second film was, I think, at least as compelling as the first one had been.

I think there's a parallel here. The scale of the church's warfare is immense, far further than we can ever comprehend – through the ages and through the centuries and through the nations of the world. We see only a corner of it. In this congregation we're lucky, we see much more of a corner, a much bigger corner of that field than many congregations do that often feel themselves to be totally isolated, carrying on a lonely battle as if there was no warfare going on at all. As if the world was empty of combatants, nobody else engaged and they wondering why indeed they bothered to get engaged at all. And then a day like this comes. It's the First of November. It's All Saints Day. And it seems to me that this is a splendid day for me to be taking my farewell of Mayfield. For it is one day that ensures that my attention and yours doesn't become focused down upon single events and localities or upon short-term memories, let alone upon certain people. It's All Saints Day. Today of all days, the lens is wide focused and people and places and events come into their proper perspective. So our theme is that.

Two weeks ago after a morning service, a lady in this congregation said to me, "I wonder what you might take as your text for your last Sunday with us?" And she said, "I thought it might well be Ephesians 3, 18." "But," she said, "you used it today instead." Well it could have indeed been the text for today. You remember it. Paul said, "I pray that you may have your roots and foundation in love so you, together with all God's people, may have the power to understand how broad and long, how high and deep is Christ's love. Yes, may you come to know his love, although it can never be fully known and so be completely filled with all the fullness of God." What I think we need often is to discover the sheer spaciousness, the sheer breadth of what we observe and proclaim and live by, the magnitude of the Gospel. What John, in his own little, lonely cell on that rocky island of Patmos, recognised and discovered when he realised he was not alone. He talked about the thousands and millions of angels and all the living creatures in heaven and earth, in the world below and in the sea, all living beings in the universe and all of them were singing. So let's think for a moment, and let me try to be a little more tabloid than usual, of one or two areas of this magnitude.

Think of the geographical span of the Gospel – if you like, the universality of the church. The church is in every part of the world. The word 'ecumenical' means nothing to do with theology or ecclesiology; it means simply, 'worldwide.' During that year, a few years ago, when the church allowed me to go to many places in its name, I caught a glimpse of this as never before in four of the continents. I kept harking back and returning to, as more than once since I have done here, that tremendous hymn that says "As o'er each continent and island the dawn leads on another day, the voice of prayer is never silent nor dies the strain of praise away."

Our own, as it were, tendrils of responsibility in this place go far. We used to talk of the significance of that little corner of the world called Palestine, that little province in the Roman world. No doubt what American politicians today would be saying about Arkansas, Roman politicians of that day would be saying about Palestine – it was poor, insignificant, non-influential and for anybody coming out of it, surely his credentials should be questioned? But, of course, we have come to recognise that Palestine was in fact the strategic heart of the ancient world. The great continents as then known, Asia, Europe, Africa, all converged into that little area. There the light shone and there the Messiah of God came. We might not talk quite so confidently of the convergence now because since then we know that the heart of Christian dynamic has often been in the New World and probably still is, and indeed in the Pacific Rim, but then it was true that Palestine was the heart of the world.

Mayfield is worldwide. It's not just that there are people in this church, and I suspect in this church today, from many parts of Africa, from Korea, from the United States, from New Zealand, from South Africa – and they contribute so richly to the worship and life of this place – but it's that there are so many people in many parts of the world whose awareness is of a home church which is this building and this place. In New Zealand, in Japan where one of our members is due to have her first baby in the next two weeks, in Eastern Europe, in Latin America, in California, in Texas. So many people in all these various places and in central Africa, too. The church, even our church here, is worldwide. Chinese children sing in their Sunday Schools hymns that we've heard sung in ours. In my car, I have a tape of Chinese Sunday School children whom I heard singing the hymns that we ourselves teach our children to sing. The magazine this month of the Seventh Day Adventist Church, that has come from the United States, gives a map of the world and of the areas where Adventists are at work: quite, as it were, cold-bloodedly set about their global outreach. It tells of the proportion of Seventh Day Adventists in each of the countries where they are, and the names of the countries where as yet they are not, but intend to be. An astonishing, and maybe from our standpoint, slightly disturbing picture, of the spread of their branch of faith, but they do at least see globally and think globally, and on All Saints Day so assuredly should we.

It's not just the geographical span of the Gospel. If you like, it's the span of the variety of the churches. One thing that we're discovering, even in our own part of the city here, in the Newington Churches Council, is how we are able to understand, meet with, talk with, worship with, members of our other churches. Late last night the priest up at St Columba's, Dan Foley, phoned to say he couldn't be here today, but wishing me and us all the goodwill and blessing of his people and of him himself – and he's not the only one who does that.

In Dunblane there was a conference of the Standing Committee of Edinburgh Churches Together, which is the name now for the successor of the old Edinburgh Churches Council, and we were trying to think really of how we could express what we stood for. We found a number of words for what we in Edinburgh are looking for and what we're seeking. In the end of our two days, it was the Roman Catholic Archbishop who found words that we were happy to adopt. We defined it as follows: 'Edinburgh Churches Together exists as a sign to the people of Edinburgh of the love and forgiveness of Christ.' Now, I like that. 'Edinburgh Churches Together exists as a sign to the people of Edinburgh of the love and forgiveness of Christ.' This is what we must work for locally as well as universally. To recognise the span of the churches, the way that other people who have many emphases different from our emphases, who worship in different forms from us, are yet part of the one body, that we may share our vision with one another, have our visions corrected by one another and be enriched by one another.

On All Saints Day too, should we not be thinking about the span of cultures that are represented, or ought to be represented, within our understanding of the church? This week, indeed today, there begins the mission to Edinburgh University called 'The Case for Christianity.' Some of us can look back to our student days when we were very much involved in organising or working for student missions, university missions. The climate may well be less congenial, colder now, than it was then for us, but nevertheless the present mission to Edinburgh is being addressed by people from significant areas of university culture and different disciplines. The communion of saints demands of us that we recognise the insight of the scientists and the poets and the artists and the astronomers and the film makers and the accountants – bless them – and the engineers, the musicians and many others. To recognise their glimpse of what this world is for and what matters in it. How its various aspects, often mysterious and daunting and forbidding but enthralling to others, are related to one another, and how the Christ, the agent of creation, is, we believe, involved in them all. The theologians, of course, have a role to play. Perhaps not least in systematising the insights, recognising the vision that those others have seen. But the cultures themselves must speak for themselves in their own languages. And people who would never come inside a church, but who have sharpened insight, understanding sensitivities, which are given by God, must be acknowledged, seen by us, and shared by us.

And, I suppose, with this sense of culture comes a thing that we're not often allowed to talk about, which is the wide span of, if you like, social background that is, or should be, represented within the church. Ours is a stratified church socially because ours is a stratified society socially. Where we live tends to reflect who we are and where we worship and even how we worship. There are many Edinburghs, very different. Hardly ever meeting, not aware of each other. There are rich and there are poor, not in material terms only. Those most affluent in those terms can be the most impoverished in true spirituality and awareness of the Gospel. Let me be specific. We have a link with Kaimes Lockart Memorial Church and our responsibility at the moment, whatever other forms of shared responsibility we may claim to accept, includes that. In our congregation over the last twelve months, there's been a significant increase in participation with that, our sister church. But perhaps we need a greater commitment there too. The Gospel is for the well-heeled in their often desperate bankruptcy in spiritual values. But it's also for the homeless and for the destitute in more obvious ways. And we have them too on our doorstep.

Will you remember, too, and maybe I could have referred to this earlier, the span of a congregation's own tradition. Last Sunday morning there was a lady in church who was once a member of Mayfield, and now lives furth of Scotland, as we like to say, and she wrote me a letter this week about what it felt like to be back and the sense of nostalgia and the curious memories that it evoked. The old light, she said, that used to hang over the pulpit and the effect of this light and the red and gold furnishing behind the table, especially on dark evenings when the other lights used to be turned off during sermons. The old choir pews and the choir console. They must have been very cluttered, she thought, though she hadn't remembered it at the time. And she mentioned names, including one of someone who's in church today. She said it was almost like stepping into a time warp. She said she'd once heard the Communion of Saints likened to the spectators in a football stadium encouraging the players on the field and the Sunday service was rather like that. Well good, I'm glad it was.

Maybe we should always be aware of the people who were before us or whose names sometimes are on the credits on the windows, or in the histories that sometimes we turn to, of what happened here. I've sometimes used the expression that you feel that his church is so impregnated with prayer that if you squeeze the pillars, prayers would come forth. So may it always be. But will you think of the span of ages, not in the short, very short, history of this place, but of the Christian church itself. When John Baillie, that prince of Scottish churchmen, compiled his *Diary of Readings*, and that's a wonderful book if you don't know it, he included a passage from Gregory Dix. It was this:

> To those who know a little of Christian history, probably the most moving of all the reflections it brings is not reports of the great events and the well-remembered saints but of those innumerable millions of entirely obscure, faithful men and women, everyone with his or her own individual hopes and fears and joys and sorrows and loves, and sins and temptations and prayers, once every bit as vivid and alive as ours, as mine are now. They have left no slightest trace in the world, not even a name, but have passed to God utterly forgotten by men. Yet each of them once believed and prayed as I believe and pray and found it hard and grew slack and sinned and repented and fell again . . . There's a little ill-spelled, ill-carved rustic epitaph of the Fourth Century from Asia Minor: "Here sleeps the blessed Chione, who has found Jerusalem for she prayed much". Not another word is known of Chione, some peasant woman who lived in that vanished world of Christian Anatolia. But how lovely, if all that should survive after sixteen centuries was that one had prayed much, so that the neighbours who saw all one's life were sure one must have found Jerusalem! What did the Sunday Eucharist in her village church every week for a lifetime mean to the blessed Chione and to the millions like her then and every year since?

Maybe that letter I got during the week reflects something of what the Eucharist or, as we call it, the Lord's Supper or Holy Communion, can mean and has meant through the centuries to many people. You see, what we do in Mayfield is of little importance, and yet it can have influence under God more than we shall ever know. Our faithfulness, our love for one another, our love of our fellow men and women – it is these that release the power of God for this ailing world. This is what we too seldom are aware of, that on this day there must be the great crowd of witnesses in the stadium watching us, and as hour passes hour, day passes day, the Mexican wave of encouragement comes from them all.

I am very proud to have been a member of Mayfield, and I hope you are proud so to be and to continue to be amid all the changes that will come upon you. The church without change would be a sad church. This congregation has, I believe, done many good things. But we here are not really important in ourselves but only as part of the whole body of Christ through the world and through the ages. When I was typing this sermon in my own quite unique brand of typing which many of you know, I realised that for the Church of Scotland I used the abbreviation, capital C, small o, capital S, CoS, "Church of Scotland," but I would like to think I would use it also now of that great reality which today we celebrate, the Communion of Saints, because that is the ultimate thing and that is what we are called to serve in, to remember and to look forward to.

May God bless you in all your undertakings for him until one day, like all earthly human, transient names, the name Mayfield will be no more and the name of Christ alone be exalted. In the words of the writer to the Hebrews – "Until we are come unto Mount Zion and unto the city of the living God, the heavenly Jerusalem and to an innumerable company of angels, to the General Assembly and company of the first born who are written in Heaven, and to God the judge of all, and to the spirits of just men made perfect and to Jesus" – to whom with the Father and the Holy Spirit be honour, glory, might, dominion now and for ever.

# COMMITMENT – THE PRIORITY OF THE NEEDY AND THE CALL TO MISSION

"He found the place where it is written: The spirit of the Lord is upon me because he has chosen me to bring Good News to the poor. He has sent me to proclaim liberty to the captives and recovery of sight to the blind. To set free the oppressed and announce that the time has come when the Lord will save his people. And then he closed the book and he sat down and he said 'And now it's all happening today.' " (Luke 4: 18)

There is always a problem about, as they say, preaching to the converted, telling people what needs to be done who are already up to their necks in seeking to do it. I don't know any body of people who can be guaranteed to rise to a challenge and to respond to appeals better than this congregation does and to show commitment when it is asked for. And that's a problem, because it is possible when the challenges keep coming and the appeals keep coming and the heart rending pictures keep being presented, quite frankly, to get weary of well doing. When the needs seem to be overwhelming and the appeals come in thick and fast and fresh commitment once again is requested.

I think 'commitment' is perhaps a word to note in this regard, it's so much used, it's a good word; it's such a good word, such a fashionable word nowadays that you're almost afraid to use it. What does 'commitment' mean? Well, it means different things in different senses. To a football coach or a football manager, it means quite simply getting stuck in, and getting stuck in more than the other side so that the fifty-fifty balls are won in more cases than they are lost. It means totality of effort. In another context it means continuity of effort, that is, not just a one-off situation, there's got to be continuing perseverance in it, not just one concert for the poor of the earth or of one corner of the earth, because by the time the concert has been organised and paid for, then the need is perhaps even greater somewhere else.

Commitment has to be for good and that is the hurdle for many people in a number of fields. Marriage is one. How can I commit myself to one person for an indefinite number of years when I shall be constantly changing and the other person may be constantly changing? Is commitment a realistic request to be made in undertaking some post – it may be a post of responsibility in society, it may be eldership in the church? So you may hear, "I can do it for a time, but don't expect me to go indefinitely". Commitment means totality of effort, it may mean continuity of effort and it may sometimes be taken to mean exclusiveness of involvement. This is it, among so many things that I could be asked to do, this is the one thing that I am prepared to give myself to because if I do, then I'll have to block off other things and not everybody always understands that. Even people with one tremendous concern within the life of the Church may not always understand that the particular, almost exclusive, interest that they have is not necessarily shared by everybody to the same extent, and that other people have their own exclusive interests and nobody can spread abroad over all the interests that are presented to us. And yet commitment has to mean that you drop something in order adequately, or as adequately as you know, to give yourself wholeheartedly to something else.

I have heard people say in the past, "You know, there was this wonderful cause and there are goodness knows how many hundreds of people in the congregation and only X number of people came to this – that's terrible." It's difficult for them to understand that the particular, almost exclusive, interest that they have is not necessarily shared by everybody to the same extent, and that other people have their own exclusive interests and nobody can spread abroad over all in the interests that are presented to us. And yet commitment has to mean that you drop something in order adequately, or as adequately as you know, to give yourself wholeheartedly to something else.

There are so many requirements, so many appeals, so many challenges. I think we have to ask: are there any areas of general commitment that for most of us might seem to be absolute commitment, absolute commands which seem to be built into the very fabric of discipleship? I say most of us, for I know very well that there are some people who do have a prior commitment, a prior involvement; it may be facing an impossible domestic situation, it may be coping with one wholly dependent person who demands attention twenty-four hours a day, it may be in serving one small and little known corner of God's Kingdom and doing it often without recognition, it may be overcoming one weakness, or climbing one mountain. But for most of us whose lives are not subjected to that kind of exceptional demand, are there points of commitment that are part of Christian discipleship? I think there may be two. One is quite simply the claim of the poor. Jesus said: "This is why I have come, this is why the spirit has been given to me. This is why I have been chosen to bring Good News to the poor." Quite a number of you will be going round with Christian Aid envelopes this week. I suspect many of you are not looking forward to it, and not least because of what I have said, because there are so many demands made upon people these days.

There is something called 'charity fatigue' which has emerged in recent months. Too many emergencies, too many demands, until we almost don't want to know. The Kurds and the 'Simple Truth' may be overtaken by the Bangladeshis, and the Africans have been there all the time and will still be there. Concerns and appeals compete with each other and we don't know how to compare, to find out what we should do. The problem is simply too great. What are the figures: a million Kurdish refugees, four million Bangladeshi survivors from the cyclone, twenty-seven million at hazard in Africa? There's always the unease created by reports that some the statutory agencies may not always seem to be operating as effectively or as altruistically as they ought to be doing.

The other expression is 'aid weariness.' There's a remarkable and compelling letter this week from the onetime Secretary of the Church of Scotland's Board of World Mission and Unity; Chris Wigglesworth recognized how the aid weariness could affect our view of the needs in Ethiopia, Etritrea, Sudan, Somalia and those countries to the South. He pointed out that help through Christian Aid's partners is making a difference there, as it is for Kurdish refugees and Bangladeshi survivors. What is being done may seem so minimal but it is being done and he asked that people who are seeking to work for Christian Aid this week should not feel apologetic about it, but should recognise that, through that medium, which is one of the most respected and efficiently and economically organised of all aid bodies, aid is being funnelled to the places where, however tormenting the decision, the need seems at any particular time to be greatest. The Women's Guild has sent over £18,000 to Christian Aid for Africa. The Board has just sent special grants of £5,000 – how tiny – to the Church of

Bangladesh and £2,400 to the Malawi Church of Central Africa Presbyterian, for the victims of flood disaster. These may be small amounts and they are small amounts in terms of the need, but they are sacrificial amounts. It is said that they are of real use to our partner churches and they are.

Don't let's be afraid or ashamed to ask or to give. I would like to suggest that every one of us this week might take seriously those lifestyle leaflets which were circulated with Mayfield News at the beginning of the month. Even if we haven't done so before, to examine them and to recognise that they help us to remember our own richness, our unthinking blessings, and may be even that we should decide here and now that we will do something of that kind before the intercession prayers that will come up in fifteen minutes, otherwise we may find it difficult properly to pray when the time comes. You see, I am aware that we think: "My little piece, what difference will it make, will it even be noticed?"

Can I just say one or two things about this, that seem to me to be so obvious though I don't always live by them. The first thing is that every little does help. If something buys one load of bread, or one load of grain, then that is something for somebody, and it may just be the difference between someone's death and someone's – for the time being – survival. The second thing is that voluntary giving, such as Christian Aid and so on, shames governments, which are far more sensitive to public opinion than often we think. And then the reverse of this. When you give, you begin to care. "Where your treasure is," said Jesus, "there will your heart be also." When we have given something slightly sacrificially to a certain need and have done it genuinely – with concentration and at some cost – then we have a personal involvement in that situation, which changes us. The corollary to that is that the kind of lifestyle that we seek to adopt does matter. It reflects our own thoughts and our own caring. When we give, we are changed, though it may not seem to show. If enough of us are moved to see things through the eyes of the world's poor then our own society will be altered in its attitudes. And I would say this, that, if we have a choice, there is a strong case for using the voluntary agencies that have a track record of good management. Some of the international and internationally funded bodies have a got a record of providing a gravy train for those who operate them, and whose own lifestyles as a result are curiously and sometimes embarrassingly suspect.

So, I am saying that if there are imperatives, if there are commitments, that are built into our discipleship, one is the commitment which Jesus put at the top of his programme, Good News of hope for the poor. Charity, if you like, whatever the motives may be. The Old Testament is full of it. The Psalms talk about God having as his priority the care of the poor and of the widowed. The Psalms and the Book of Proverbs are all full of the importance of this and Jesus himself said a great deal about money and money well used. And we are to help with imagination, not just as a duty, not just as a casual routine. The most generous people to the poor, it always seems are the poor themselves. Ask anyone who has shaken a collecting box in the streets in what area of the city they would like to do the collecting and where the response will be most genuine, most understanding. The most effective giving is when we identify with the situation, not just to duty off the sense of guilt that we have, our own unease at having so much.

There is a second imperative which, I think, is to spread the Good News. This is built in to our discipleship. The Good News is relief for the poor, it is the work of the Kingdom, it is a whole world of deliverance that was set out there. Deliverance is a very wide thing, it is profoundly a religious thing, it is stating the liberation that is within the Gospel itself. It is the whole question of communication.

There is not enough talk in our society about the need for religious living and religious response and, indeed, the place of worship. It is not enough on the part of some of us sharing with others what we may have found to be satisfying to ourselves. It is very clear if only once a year every member of this congregation introduced one new member and every family introduced just one other family, what there would be. There would be embarrassment of space, there would be multiplication of resources, possibly multiplication of staff, there would certainly be rejoicing and there would be fulfilment of our own discipleship and a new discovery of what the wealth of the Gospel is.

If every student or householder who has found some kind of guideline to life through worship here said something by way of encouragement and invitation to another student or householder, then the Church in Scotland would have a prospect of surviving into the second half of next century. It is not just numbers for the sake of numbers. It is when numbers keep leaking away that all the life of the Church becomes debilitated because fewer people can provide less for the rest of society including the poor of this country and the needy abroad. It is not just a question of trying to build up numbers, it is trying to build up the body of Christ to do the work that the body of Christ is there to do. And the fact is that we are not doing it.

We will all have good reasons for not doing so – our own shyness, our own limitations, but if the Church itself means something to us, then I think we have no option. We can't really, any of us as individuals, chicken out of it. There is always someone who has no regular Church connection at all, someone whose connection elsewhere has virtually lapsed, somebody who has moved into an area and is waiting to see if someone will speak. The value to ourselves is infinite too. There is this personal satisfaction for ourselves, there is joy in heaven for Jesus, and there is a deepening of quality of our own resources for serving the Kingdom. So if some of us are going out distributing Christian Aid envelopes and maybe wishing we weren't, while others have offered – and in some cases even the same people – to go out and distribute letters of invitation in part of the parish and may be finding it not easy to go back, nevertheless we should recognise that we are in fact doing something which all of us should be doing which is part of the work of the Kingdom of Christ. Call it 'evangelism' if you like, though the visitation which we undertake in the parish is specifically not seen to be evangelistic. It is just quite simply a mission of friendship and of goodwill and of information.

Mission is far wider, after all, than evangelism and it is something that we cannot leave to others. The word 'evangelism' creates a feeling of unease in the minds of some people. There are many who feel that the kind of mass evangelism which has come from America through the years – sometimes most effectively, sometimes less than effectively – is not always the kind of thing that we want to see identified with our own Church's approach to mission. And yet, if we do feel that, and if, for example, we have misgivings about mass evangelical rallies ,we have no alternative but to say, "Well if that is the case, if we don't feel that's the way evangelism should be conducted, then what is the right kind of evangelism for ourselves?"

If you don't like a Murrayfield rally, then what do you like? If you don't like people being asked to come forward and make a commitment while the organ plays, then how do you want people to make a commitment to Christ? Or is it that we don't care if people make a commitment to Christ and to the Christian way at all? That we are content to say, "Well, let them go on in their own way and find their own way to Christ if they can and if they want and we will politely stand back and wave them in when they arrive, but we won't go out and seek them."

If that had happened in the early days of the Church, within thirty years of the resurrection there would have been no Christian Church at all. Then or ever. So if you are left cold by what Billy Graham and the traditional United States type of evangelists say, you have to ask yourself, do you really believe something that is sufficiently precious to you, real to you, that you would feel sorry for somebody else if they failed to discover it too? In other words do you and I have something that we passionately want to share with other people? And if you haven't – let me ask you this, if you haven't invited someone to share in some aspect of Christian life and worship, if you haven't ever – or at least in the past year – invited someone to accompany you, even to a morning service or, perhaps better sometimes, to an evening service, or to a discussion group, then why?

There are certain aspects of discipleship which are open to some and maybe not to others. Paul says: "Some are called to be this and some are called to be that and some are called to be something else, and not everybody is called to be everything." But there are I think certain areas of commitment which are built in to discipleship and they are related to what Jesus himself set forth. I believe that, in the light of his proclamation of his commissioning, of his programme, these areas must be seen to be paramount. One is the priority of the needy, and the other is the call to mission.

In so far as we feel a response to these and in so far as we seek to dedicate ourselves to respond to them, then, after the offering that we make to the ordinary life of the Church, our own intercessions today may take on a new dimension of reality and our lives this week may find a new depth of joy in our commitment to Christ.

# COMPETITION AND CHARACTER

This is a week when competition raises its ugly, or its exciting, head. I think there are one or two gaps in the church this morning where people normally, ninety-nine percent of the time, would be, but those people have today wandered down somewhere in East Lothian for some reason or another. And there are other people who are not here because they graduated from University this week and have gone home or have gone off on holiday or have gone somewhere to celebrate.

This is the competition time and that can be, to some extent, quite an exciting time. There are those of you who are young enough to remember what it was like at your first Sunday School picnic – no, you can't! Others of you may remember small children with you on your first Sunday School picnic and some of you at the last Sunday School picnic will have observed that, in the beginners' race, or whatever it's called, the first problem is simply to get the competitors, not to leap out of the starting blocks, but to face in the right direction. Once you've got them faced in the right direction, you say, "When someone waves a hand, or drops a handkerchief, you've to run as fast as you possibly can to those people standing away in the distance." And you more or less get the response, "Why?" And the answer is, "Because you've got to run faster than the other people and beat them." That makes no sense at all to them, and maybe it does make no sense at all in our world, but, anyhow, they are prodded from behind and gradually and slowly and with total lack of enthusiasm, they waddle off in the other direction. They haven't learnt this art of being competitive in this competitive world.

But you do learn it and you learn it at school. You've got to do not just as well as you can, you've got to do better if you can than the other people and you'll maybe get a prize. Or you learn it at mini-rugby or something, where, at far too early an age, dads, and even mums, jump up and down screaming on the touch line telling people to get tore in. Competitiveness is the name of the game and it is for many of us for the rest of our lives. Some of us even beyond the time when we think the competition is over find that, tragically and sadly sometimes, the competition is still there and we've lost out on it.

During this month people find themselves watching other people playing games in a curious kind of way, people who themselves could never play tennis, or haven't done so for years, are enthralled by the TV box shape of a tennis court. People who couldn't come within a hundred miles of shooting a birdie, except in their fantasising dreams, are hung on the screen watching other people doing so. So effortlessly, so magically, that you feel you might even be prepared to have another shot at it. Wimbledon, Muirfield, Barcelona. The fact is that we're not really interested sometimes in which millionaire is going to overtake which other millionaire in the final run in. Which of them is going to hit a little ball with a little stick the fewest number of times. What we are interested in is how they respond to what we are aware of, which is stress, tension and how you really react when as we say, the chips are down. And whether they have the character, because competition is very often about character. What sort of people they really are. How they respond when they have to take a second service at match point. Or the ten foot putt that normally they could do with their eyes closed, but under the strain of tension, how will they respond?

We know about Tom McKean and Liz McColgan and Linford Christie and that wonderful man Kriss Akabussi. We do not so easily identify with the great African middle distance runners from Ethiopia or Kenya, who themselves will do incredible things, and yet somehow we'll marvel at fortitude, strength, stamina, perseverance, character. For the understanding of these things in one another and in ourselves is, I think, part of our own religious experience, and that is why the experience even of the earliest Christians, and even of our Lord himself, has its own magnetic quality as we observe these in the Scriptures.

You remember Marathon and the man who ran 26 miles 385 yards from the battle to convey the news. We're going to read the story of an equivalent marathon that took place almost four hundred years earlier than the battle in Greece: the passage is in Second Samuel, Chapter 18. You can read it or you can listen to it and I want you to imagine at one point that I'm standing up, straining my eyes into the distance, down the Jordan Valley, waiting for someone to appear, just as a television commentator, from his very high gantry, will be waiting amid the buzz of expectancy to see who the first runner will be to come through the gates of the stadium in the marathon and to see if he'll be all by himself or if, just possibly, there may be somebody on his heels so that the last circuit of the area will be quite decisive.

The context of this is that King David, the great King of the Jewish people, in his latter years faced competition from, of all people, his own son Absalom, whom he loved very, very greatly. Absalom raised a rebellion against David, and David and his friends had to flee from Jerusalem, their capital, and for a time they took up residence in another city called Mahanaim. Joab, who was a very blood-thirsty general who by this time fought David's wars for him, had gone out to fight against the rebel forces of David's own son, Abasalom. And David was waiting for news to come of what the outcome of the battle would be. He must have hoped, as all the people around him hoped, that Absalom would be defeated, but above all things what David was concerned about was that Absalom himself, his own son, should be safe. But in the battle Absalom was defeated and was killed.

The watchman on the tower was watching and waiting for news and David was sitting where he couldn't see what was happening. He was sitting between the inner gate and the outer gate of the ramparts of that city and the watchman would convey news to him when it came. Of course, if the watchman saw a little crowd of bedraggled people, a little group of refugees on the skyline, he would know it was bad news, that David had been defeated, but if it was only one man bringing news, then that could be good news, but what kind of good news would it be? So the story begins in Joab's camp before the news is conveyed. Second Samuel, 18: 19:

> Then Ahimaaz, son of Zadok, who was the priest, said to Joab, "Let me run to the king with the good news that the Lord has saved him from his enemies." "No," Joab said, "Today you will not take any good news. Some other day you may do it, but not today, for the king's son is dead." Then he said to his Sudanese slave – Ethiopian really, a middle distance runner – "Go and tell the king what you have seen." And the slave bowed and ran off. Ahimaaz insisted, "I don't care what happens, please let me take the news also." "Why do you want to do it, my son?" Joab asked, "You will get no reward for it." "Whatever happens" Ahimaaz said again, "I want to go." "Then go", Joab said. So Ahimaaz

ran off down the road, through the Jordan Valley and soon he passed the slave, overtook him. David was sitting in the space between the inner and outer gates of the city. The watchman went up to the top of the wall and stood on the roof of the gateway and looked out and he saw a man running alone. And he called down and he told the king, and the king said, "If he's alone, he's bringing good news." The runner came nearer and nearer. And then the watchman saw another man running alone and he called down to the gatekeeper, "Look, there's another man running." And the king answered, "This one also is bringing good news." And the watchman said, "I can see that the first man is running like Ahimaaz. "He's a good man," the king said, "And he is bringing good news." And Ahimaaz called out a greeting to the king and threw himself down to the ground before him and said, "Praise the Lord your God who has given you victory over the men who rebelled against your majesty." "Is the young man Absalom safe?" the king asked. And Ahimaaz answered, "Sir, when your officer Joab sent me, I saw a great commotion but I couldn't tell what it was." "Stand over there," the king said. And he went over and stood there. Then the Sudanese slave arrived and said to the king. "I have good news for your majesty. Today the Lord has given you victory over all who rebelled against you." "Is the young man Absalom safe?" the king asked. The slave answered, "I wish that what has happened to him would happen to all your enemies, sir, and to all who rebel against you." The king was overcome with grief. He went up to the room over the gateway and wept and as he went he cried, "Oh my son, my son Absalom, Absalom my son, if only I had died in your place, my son. Absalom, my son."

Which of the two men won the race? Well Ahimaaz was the faster, but Ahimaaz wasn't the victor in the end because at the last moment, when he had to say what he had to say and do what he had to do, his heart failed him his courage failed him. He failed. He came short in character. It's not a question of being able to run faster than other people. It's the kind of character you have and how you run your race through your life that matters and whether you do what you know you ought to do and have to do, even if it's difficult, even when the going is rough.

One of the hardest things in life is to accept defeat and to do it gracefully. Another hard thing is to accept victory and to do it humbly. I was once in a church in California. It was a huge church called the Crystal Cathedral, made of glass. It was a church whose minister, Robert Schuler, a splendid minister, would broadcast weekly to millions of people across America. That day they had a guest speaker, or a guest interviewee. He was the fastest man on earth, Carl Lewis. People were looking forward to him coming, but wondering if he would turn up. At the slot where he was to appear, the minister had to look around and say, "I'm sorry, but Carl Lewis doesn't seem to have come." And people said, "Well, he often lets you down like that."

To be a victor is a very exposed thing because people's expectations are so high of you and you've to sign every autograph and be kind and accepting and modest and humble, even when you're totally worn out. But that's one of the prizes of success and people who win great triumphs may just have to be careful that they don't become too conceited. If you don't win, then of course it's equally hard to put a brave face on it and maybe even to congratulate the person who has won and to try to conceal the disappointment in you own heart.

I know one or two people from overseas who had to get a particularly high qualification in order to have their grant from their own Third World country continued. They did the best they could and they got a very adequate degree pass, but not enough. So now they'll have to go home and their friends here will be disappointed for them and their friends back home will be disappointed too. Character comes when you're faced with having to say, "I didn't make it." Am I then just going to give it all up? Am I just going to hide my head under a parapet, or am I going to show the measure of self-discipline that is needed to pick oneself off the ground and say, "Well, there's a lot living still to be done?"

Some of you at school will know this, when other people so effortlessly seem to win prizes just because they have that kind of mind, and you've worked jolly hard but have nothing to show for it. If you've done the best that you possibly know how to, then you have done well enough and the honour is due to you. In the ancient games in Greece, the winner of the races was given a large cheque to spend. He would be given a garland of ivy or oak or bay leaves, depending which games they were. Valueless, and yet the proudest thing he could have to wear. He'd go back to his home city and he would take the garland and he would lay it before the altar of his god, because he would say that it was his god who'd enabled him to do this and he wanted to pay it back to the god who had helped him.

I don't think that Paul was a very athletic man. Allegedly he was quite small and some people said he was bandy legged. But he was very self-disciplined and he ordered his life well for the sake of Christ whom he loved. And so I'm going to ask you to read with me a letter that Paul wrote to the people at Corinth, who were mad about sports, and he used the illustration of sport for them.

In 1 Corinthians 9: 19, Paul said,

"I'm a free man, nobody's slave; but I make myself everybody's slave in order to win as many people as possible. While working with the Jews, I live like a Jew in order to win them; and even though I myself am not subject to the law of Moses, I live as though I were when working with those who are, in order to win them. In the same way, when working with Gentiles, I live like a Gentile, outside the Jewish law, in order to win Gentiles. This does not mean that I don't obey God's law; I'm really under Christ's Law. Among the weak in faith I become weak like one of them, in order to win them. So I become all things to all men, that I may save some of them by whatever means are possible. All this I do for the Gospel's sake, in order to share in its blessings. Surely you know that many runners take part in a race, but only one of them wins the prize. Run, then, in such a way as to win the prize. Every athlete in training submits to strict discipline, in order to be crowned with a wreath that will not last; but we do it for one that will last for ever. That is why I run straight for the finishing line; that is why I am like a boxer who does not waste his punches. I harden my body with blows and bring it under complete control, to keep myself from being disqualified after having called others to the contest." We can't all win. But we can all do the best that we are capable of doing for our Lord, Jesus Christ.

# THE UNCHANGING GOSPEL
# IN A CHANGING WORLD

(Preached at Holy Communion)

"If a man loves Me he will keep My words and My Father will love him and we will come unto him and make our abode with him." (John 14: 23)

Ours is a curiously insecure world at the moment, more than many of us remember it being, which is why a promise like that is significant because it offers, in the name of Christ, permanency and stability. For in our world these don't exist. The authorities qualify their statements or do U-turns upon them. The specialists hedge their bets. Convictions are shaded and moral standards are put back into the melting pot. Political alignments are spectacularly re-jigged. The polls and the prophets are more than usually unsure of themselves and the trumpets give an uncertain sound. I suppose we crave a sense of permanence, knowing that things change but needing the conviction that change may be for the better – and, above all, that change is an element in the Christian pilgrimage – among the hazards in Christian life are immobility and too great a desire for permanence.

Remember the Last Supper. Jesus' words at the Last Supper reflect a swirling mist of uncertainty. There are going to be comings and goings, and whence and where are not carefully spelt out. All the disciples are told is that there's much in store that will be good but cannot be spoken of yet. And the one certain thing in all of that is that there will yet be a settled place and a settled relationship. "My Father and I will", as it were, "put our roots down and make our abode" with the person who loves God and loves his words. That is even more than the greatly beloved words in Revelation where Jesus says, "I stand at the door and knock. If anyone hears My voice and opens the door, I will come into him and sup with him and he with me." It's more than just saying He will come and eat with, have a meal with, us. It is: My Father will come and settle himself in that person's home and live there permanently. That is permanence indeed.

Maybe the Holy Communion service is increasingly, for us, set against that pattern of uncertainty. It is timeless. The words and actions follow a pattern that we've inherited and, on the whole, are at home with and want to have conserved to us. In football terms, the build up is as it always was and the shots are on target but the goal posts so often seem to have moved and the environment has changed. And yet we call this the climax of our Christian worship. Here we have the continuity and the security, if you like, and the stability.

Remember that it may always have been so in the context of this sacrament and of what preceded it. For the forerunner of the Holy Communion, as we know, and from which its pattern derived, was the Jewish Passover which was set in the same kind of context, for the swirling mists were certainly there. These people were a slave people with no great expectations, but at least they knew that they had a kind of security – they were settled, domesticated people, hardly remembering the conditions of those who had gone before them. For those who had gone before them had been always on the march. It was in their tradition – how Father Abraham had once set out into the unknown, not knowing whither he went. How Jacob had set out on his own and pitched his lonely bedspread beneath the stars at Bethel. How Joseph and his brothers had first discovered the alien land of Egypt. The prospect of moving again was, by this time, after all these years, for some of them creating disquiet and unease. Nobody quite knew what tomorrow would bring. And yet this is the climax of the Old Testament, for I think it comes thus early in the Book of Exodus. It revolves around a meal, which is a foreshadowing of our symbolic meal which is a meal for travellers, for after you've eaten this meal you've to be prepared for moving. The words of the Lord to Moses are these, in Exodus, "You're to eat it quickly for you're to be dressed for travel, with your sandals on your feet and your stick in your hand." And on that very night the first-born of Egypt died. And on that very night, the Pharaoh called Moses, "Get out, get out, the lot of you. Go and serve the Lord as you asked to do." And off they went. That took tremendous commitment, to up sticks. That alone would bring them through years and years of wandering to the promised land.

Some of us are still scared, perhaps all of us, of the unfamiliar, even though we are supposed to be followers of the Christ who had no settled place to lay his head and who once said that, to be his disciples, we had to take up our cross. Some scholars have translated these words, "pull up your tent pegs and follow me." And so the roots of the Holy Communion are in a pilgrim people about to be on the march, so that logically, if we are following the example of the Passover people whose wanderings began at the very moment when God sealed to them their covenant, I suppose our engines should be running and our cars loaded to the gunwales at West Mayfield.

It is important for us to look back in this kind of way because this is the place where and the occasion on which we dare to look back on the way that we've come, the way that God has led his church through the ages. Some of us are uneasy about looking forward and some of us are uneasy about looking back. The climax of the New Testament also comes very early, it comes in the Last Supper I believe, in the forming of the new Israel and in the preparation for the momentous events of the following day, the cross itself. The events are the same. The venue has changed, the menu has not. The prospect of tomorrow has not changed either. For the disciples gathered that night in all the unease of the way they had come hitherto, thankful for much in it, but quite unsure, and Jesus almost helped to make them unsure about what would follow.

All this I wrote yesterday. I'm now going to read some words that I wrote for a sermon quite a long time ago. It bears, I think, upon this too. It was a sermon about the Holy Communion, and it said this:

> The fellowship of the Lord's table is never an end in itself. It always looks to the future. It was so on the night of its institution. The disciple band would not be there together again. They were thinking of what was to follow. Their conversation was of the ordeals, unknown and so all the more fearful, that were surely to come. And there was an atmosphere of impermanence about this and its meaning would only be seen in the future. And for Jesus himself, his thoughts and his words were likewise on what was immediately to come, the betrayal, the arrest, the torment. And on the fulfilment which only he could foresee. We can't see into the future. We don't want to see into the future. But we must do so today for this meal is in itself an act of faith that there is a future in which

Jesus is Lord. There are those who cannot look back" – I said then – "because the past was too unbearably joyful with a dear face and a dear heart that made life so different from what it now is, and they turn their eyes away. Or because they're ashamed of the past." But I said then, and would say again, "I know one place where we can dare to look forward and dare to look back and dare to live in this hour and day, and that is at the Lord's table. Don't ask what does the sacrament do, ask what you are going to do and be in the strength of Christ, for the grace of Christ is offered you for these days immediately before you. But it's not just to the immediate future that the sacrament points, it points far beyond the fullness of the Kingdom of God. Indeed it points us home to where we belong. Have you ever found difficulty in answering someone who said, "Where do you belong?" Born in this place, spent my childhood in that place, lived most of my life in this other place. The place we belong to is the place we are making for, not the place from which we've come. The world we live in is only our temporary home and we are pilgrims and strangers on earth and the sacrament of this day points us on our way.

That's a bit of a sermon that I preached on the first Communion Sunday in this church when I was minister here, on 25th June 1959, and I think I would still want to stand by what I seem to have said then. It's a very different world. A much more secure world. No four-minute warnings, no Cold War. It's a very different church. Mayfield's a different church. The Church of Scotland and the church worldwide, for better or worse, are very different. You are different, those of you who were here at that time, and that sermon betrays its date by the fact that I used the word 'you' whereas nowadays I would have said 'we.' I am a very different person to what I was then. But the words that were used then, I think, do stand. Because the Gospel is unchanging. The promise of Christ is unchanging. The power of God in the Holy Spirit is unchanging. and our confidence in him, as generations pass and as year succeeds year, dares not change because many of us have known that it is reliable, to be depended upon, and others of us are still to test it but are prepared to go out into whatever lies before us, in order to do just that.

I ended that sermon as I shall end this one, with the words that were written by one of the ministers of the Confessing Church in Germany in the Hitler years. Paul Schneider, in December 1937, shortly after he was admitted to Buchenwald concentration camp where presently he died, wrote this: "You will understand that despite the fellowship of many fellow prisoners, I can still feel lonely at times. But the good God is with me here and can make that which is far off, near. He can make this strange land my homeland. He can meet me in this world with all the power of the world to come."

And so for this short time, we sit still together in company with one another, and then, just as, in obedience to the command of Pharaoh, the people went out, scattered, never to go back to Egypt again, so we recall that, at the very end of the chapter, Jesus said suddenly, "Come on, let's go. That's enough. Let's get out of here." "Arise, let us go forth," he said. That is always our response to the Gospel, it's a response to the Communion, that here we gather at the place where, with us, the Lord assuredly is, that we then may go forth, heartened and fortified, into the world where also He is, that we may serve him all our days, to the glory of Jesus Christ our Lord.

# WHAT IS A CHRISTIAN?

I had thought of preaching on 1 John 3: 2, which begins: "My dear friends, we are now God's children, but it is not yet clear what we shall become," because this seemed to me to be important about our own conviction of where we stand and yet also about our own, in a sense, insecurity about where we're heading without the grace of God. But I decided rather to go back to the passages which we thought about last Sunday, 1 John 2: 5-6, because there's something very austere about this which comes before any of our confidence, possibly – or maybe it's the ground of our confidence. Let the words speak for themselves. "Here is the test by which we can make sure that we are in him. Whoever claims to be dwelling in him binds himself to live as Christ himself lived."

A friend of mine last week told me of a long train journey he had made in company with a couple whom he did not know, but who had with them a very severely handicapped child. And he was clearly deeply moved at the patience and the love which the parents had shown towards that little one during the whole of that journey. And he said, "It was the most Christian thing I have ever seen." The most Christian thing I have ever seen. Now, my friend who said that, is a Jew. Not a practising Jew, but one who stands up for the rights of the Jewish people, their land and their nation and their tradition, even though he never goes to the synagogue. But he didn't say it was the most Jewish thing he had ever seen or come across, or even the most humane, or even the most humanitarian. He said it was the most Christian. The word 'Christian' isn't one that he likes to use every often.

Would someone kindly tell me what is a Christian? You could write it – no, you'd better not write it – on the back page of the hymn book or of your bibles. Graffiti, however orthodox and edifying, are not encouraged! But suppose you were to write down the answer, what would you write? "A Christian is . . ." Pity you can't, because the answers would be very varied when they came back and I find that very surprising. We all ought to find it very surprising. You would think there ought to be some common definition of something so totally basic as what a Christian is, but in the New Testament there's no definition.

In fact, they were rather chary of using the word Christian, it seems. It's used very seldom in the New Testament. It's used by other people of them. "The disciples were first called Christians" – not by themselves. The disciples were first called Christians in Antioch as a kind of nickname. And when they use it of themselves it's in response to what others have said, it's in quotes always. Peter talks about, "Don't be afraid of suffering as a Christian because other people say you are a Christian, because that's part of your lot as followers of Jesus Christ." But it took a very, very long time before the standard words of the church, of the believers, the followers, the disciples, were changed into self-consciously using the word 'Christian' to speak to themselves.

You would think that a least in the days of the catechisms and of the confessions there would be a consensus, an approved definition. What does the Shorter Catechism say? Surely there must be among so many scores of questions one that says, "What is a Christian?" but there isn't. The word doesn't even appear in the index. And that useful little paperback, the Fontana Dictionary of Modern Thought has "Christian democracy" and "Christian existentialism," not 'Christian' as a noun. "Christianity" is there as "the religion based on the work and teaching of Jesus." Fair enough, we all know that. But what constitutes a Christian? Other books of reference, like the Oxford Dictionary of the Christian Church, talk about the official Roman definition of members of the church, but it says that in modern times it has tended in nominally Christian countries to lose any creedal significance and imply only what is ethically praiseworthy. And that's coming closer to what my Jewish friend, I suppose, would say about what being Christian is.

I'm pretty sure of this, that historically and for the New Testament Christians, the word 'Christian' is a term that belongs to the fellowship of the whole community, to the body rather than to the individual within it. To be Christian is to be identified with those who stand for certain things, who own a certain allegiance, who practise certain actions, who follow a certain way of life. Some of them may be magnificent at it, they may be called saints. Some of them are pretty inept at it and some of them could do better. (As the child said, "My father's a Christian but he's not doing very much about it at the moment.")

At different stages, it is the combined corporate community, including those who have earned first class honours, those who have duly performed, those on the point of having to resit if they're unlucky. They are all entitled to the word 'Christian' but to pick out individual points of standing and of status is perhaps a thing that the New Testament does not encourage us to do. Yes, we know all about the sheep and the goats. We know all about the narrow way, the little turnstile and the wide road. But we don't have a definition. Now in that sense you can justify the position of, I think, the great majority of those who belong to Christian churches and communities world-wide, who, if they were asked that question, would have no problems at all such as we might have. They would simply say, a Christian is someone who has been baptised into the church. Or some would say a Christian is one who has been baptised and confirmed into the church. And other large segments of the church wouldn't understand the difference because in the orthodox world baptism and confirmation are regarded as following immediately one after the other.

Some of us, I suppose, are in danger of being very uneasy at where I seem to be heading – maybe I am too. For some of us, I know, would totally disown Christianity as being defined by being baptised or confirmed. Some would want to make it purely a personal matter. A Christian is one who has taken Jesus Christ as his personal Saviour and Lord. I don't think the Bible is ever quite as personal as that. It does rather see the believer as one who stands among those who recognise Jesus as Saviour and Lord. And of course a personal affirmation and decision to be so is implied by that, but always there is this sense of being numbered with those who so believe and who so live.

Now, popularly, the evidence of being a Christian is what you do, not what you believe. "He's a real Christian." Like people who have in the back windows of their cars, to my constant embarrassment when I see it, "I'm a real Scot," or "I'm a real nit," or "I'm a real . . ." something, from Edinburgh or from somewhere or another. I'm a real Christian, because . . . – what? "He is a real Christian." How often have you heard it used in a negative way? "He was a real Christian, he never harmed a fly." "He was a real Christian, he never said an ill word about anyone." That would have ruled out Paul for a start. It would probably have ruled out Jesus himself who had a good many ill words to say about people: very sharp words, and words of hurt, for their healing, and for the sake of righteousness and for the sake of God, and for the honour of God.

To be a Christian is a far more positive and even more aggressive thing than simply to be ineffective and wimpish and colourless. Maybe the important thing about being a Christian is that you can't define it. You can't say this is what being a Christian is, and I am it. For there is no single definition that is adequate. You can't readily define relationships with anybody, anybody you love.

So am I not going to suggest any possible answers? Yes I am, I'm going to suggest three possible answers. Not clear-cut definitions, but just pointers to what being a Christian has been defined as by certain people.

The first derives from an American called Alfred Starrat, who gave a lot of thought to this kind of thing. The way he put it was, "Are there any minimum standards that make up a Christian's life?" And he says: "A real Christian is an individual whose life is motivated by greater love than that of the ordinary run of the population." That seems pretty loose. But then he goes on, "This love takes its origin and motive from Jesus of Nazareth." It is a love that can be demonstrated in five dimensions. Intensity: it's real and passionate. Extensity: it's wider than it would otherwise be. Duration: in other words it's not a passing enthusiasm. Purity: it's not diluted or self-seeking. And – Adequacy. I'm not sure what 'adequacy' means. I suppose it means that it works, that it's not just an idea in the mind, it's effective, practical. I'll give you these again: "This love takes its origin and motive from Jesus of Nazareth. It's a love that can be demonstrated in five dimensions – Intensity, extensity, duration, purity, adequacy." And if that's enough for one set of thoughts, then just switch off there and play around with that.

But the second set of thoughts comes from Michael Novak who's been one of the most influential Roman Catholic lay philosophers of our generation. Someone who is quoted often by Lesslie Newbigin, that great prophetic Christian. He approaches the question as a philosopher and suggests that life is built around four basic values: honesty, courage, freedom and community. The extent to which we work at these values is the extent to which we live with a sense of reality. And since all his reality is based upon Jesus Christ himself, I suppose you would take that as a working principle for what a Christian is.

The third definition, and it's not really a definition but surely it's high time we came to the words of Jesus himself, would come from the parable of the sheep and the goats in Matthew, Chapter 25. Because I think that in all the terrible things – and there have been more than the usual terrible things that have hit us from the pages of our newspapers and from the broadcasts of the media – there is this sense of asking: what is the Christian response to so many things that we feel are getting out of control, that break our hearts and we don't know what to do about? Jesus tells the story of the sheep and the goats. He suggested – and he didn't talk in terms of individuals – that it was nations, it was the community, that would find its judgement in terms of what it did with the poor and the naked and the hungry and the helpless and the needy. On one side or the other nations would stand in the last judgement, and presumably this must mean responsible, voting, articulate members of nations. It all depends upon how one responds to the needs of the neighbour.

Perhaps we should go back to 1 John, which in fact gives three tests for genuine Christianity. They can clearly be defined in those forms. First is right living. By which he means, I suppose, purity of life, that life that is strongly motivated and that, by and large, will follow a certain track right to the end, with intensity, extensity, duration, purity and adequacy. First is right living. Secondly, there is neighbour love. That comes over and over again in 1 John, which is the most demanding book in the New Testament. Terribly practical. Terribly down to earth. Neighbour love. For, quite simply, one who does not love his brother, cannot, does not, whatever he may say, love God. And, thirdly, there is right belief. The Greek word for that is 'Orthodoxy.' Right belief. By which one understands Christ as being the revelation of God, the manifestation of God, the one in whom we see who God is, what God is like, what God offers, and what God demands. And John would say that God is knowable, not a nebulous abstraction, an idea from in our own heads. God is knowable. That God has revealed himself and does reveal himself to those who seek him. Even if the way in which they find him may differ from person to person, to those who earnestly seek him, God will be found and known and his demand will be recognised and his claim and his offer will be embraced. God has revealed himself and God has made himself known adequately in Christ. That there is in the end a way to God, a way to understand him, to find him, and, at the end of the long day, to rest and find peace in him at the end of the quest.

Maybe our whole pilgrimage is a search for knowledge, for obedience, for grasping and being grasped and, at the heart of all that, there's not a series of propositions, not a series of definitions at all, but simply our looking to Jesus, the beginning and the end, the author and finisher of faith, with no sense of conceit, with no sense, as Paul says, of having arrived, but "I follow after." With the knowledge not that our hold of God in Christ is strong but that his hold of us in Christ is adequate, that his love is sufficient, not ours. That his grace is sufficient, not ours. That his commitment to us, not ours to him, is the hope and the faith and the love by which alone we live.

# WITH DEEP ROOTS AND
# STRONG FOUNDATIONS

(Preached at a Baptism)

"With deep roots and strong foundations may you be strong to grasp with all God's people what is the breadth and length and depth and height of the love of Christ and to know it, though it is beyond knowledge." (Ephesians 3: 18)

It may be that the last thing you want the minister to talk about this morning is where the country appears to be heading or to be drifting, and the dubious decisions taken, or the frightening indecisions shown, or whatever else was in 'Paper Clips' this morning or will be in the editorial columns of the Sunday heavies. That you don't want. The second thing that you may not want a minister to do either is to talk about things which have no remote point of relevance to the things you have been talking about and muttering about with your friends and over your table. All the things that we find ourselves disturbed by as we look out on the world. It's just a cop-out to talk religious words that have no reference to the world around us. It may be that the things that we want converge somehow when we see a baby – or, today, three babies and two other small people – contributing in their own particular unique way to the worship of the church this morning.

I suppose what we want, all of us, and are not quite sure how to find it, is what in Greek would be called 'evangel,' or in English 'good news,' or in the ancient English 'godspell' – gospel. But there is no evangel, no gospel, some of us would say, that does not relate to the situation in which many families in this country and in other countries, find themselves placed today. What kind of world do we bring children into? And baptise them into? And is our baptism simply a cop-out from reality, a final twitching of medieval superstition and magic? A thing that we might as well do because if we don't something worse might befall them? That if it doesn't do any good, it won't do any harm?

Today is, I think the last day that I shall be baptising children in Mayfield, three this morning and two rather older children this afternoon. That will make a total of something like a thousand children whom I've baptised at this font. Enough pretty well to fill this church nearly twice over. A few gallons of water. Quite a few words of prayer. A good many repetitions of "The Lord bless you and keep you." And what has it done for the world? What has it done for them? We don't know. And is there good news? I don't think we were singing with a great deal of gusto this morning, not as well as I've heard us sing this particular hymn ("How Great The Harvest Is") which sometimes we sing with a glorious frenzied shriek on the top notes. Maybe we were really meaning this, though – "the news did seem too good for man's believing?" Is the gospel really like that? That the spirit sent from God has brought us on our road and still the world is guiding. But guiding unobtrusively, possibly. Not always noticeably.

It may be that baptism is the point at which we find ourselves earthed into the things that are just a little bit beyond our comprehension and that thereby help us to come to terms with the things which truly are bewildering are beyond our comprehension. It's only when we are bumping along on the bottom line that I think one realises how desperately one needs some kind of wisdom, some kind of confidence, some kind of assurance that is from some force, some power beyond ourselves.

Normally we have baptisms only once a month, but the last two or three months it's been virtually every other Sunday, and I sometimes wish it was just about every Sunday because then we would always be reminded of the apparently illogical things. I would then be required (if I were going to talk about baptism) to spell out what often seems nonsense and even dangerous nonsense to some, but what I believe is true. That it's not by my wisdom, by my foresight, by my good work that I present myself for God's acceptance, but that God has done for me what I cannot conceive of happening on my own strength. That when we were inept and knew ourselves to be totally inadequate, floundering out of our depth, bumping along on the seabed, at the right moment Christ intervened. That is the Gospel. When I was unconscious, Christ plunged in to save me, to give me the kiss of life, and refused to say, "I cannot do anything for him until he comes round and understands what is going on." He didn't say that, nor,

I believe, in baptism is that said. The effectiveness of baptism may be in our wisdom, such as it is, in our goodness and faith, however dangerously minimal these may be. But they are not dependent upon anything else, anything at all in the life or experience of the children whom we thus present.

When in our society all the certainties and all the deep roots and strong foundations that Paul speaks about seem to have been unrooted or cut adrift, then it is, I think, that we're faced with what the Bible calls the scandal. Sunday is the day for scandals in the newspapers. It's very much a day for scandal in the church because a scandal means a stumbling block, something that humanly speaking we don't quite know how to cope with or overcome. Something that blocks off our logical sequence of thought and expression. Something that breaks in from outside, in fact, upon our thinking and says, this is what God has done, all undeserving, all unworthily, all unpredictably.

Baptism speaks most glaringly, most, if you like, confrontationally, of that. That when we are without strength, helpless, God can intervene. And that when we turn in our emptiness and our bewilderment and our fear and our uncertainty (and, I believe, the Bible speaks at least as much in this regard to nations as it does to individuals), then God can do that which of ourselves we cannot. But it's because we see the Gospel not in terms of some kind of pseudo-magical incantation of words, as some people might think baptism was. Or some kind of nostalgic sentimentalism as to how it once was, the family pews and young men and maidens going up to church, and all of us secure that the providential hand of God was so evidently at work in society, which of course it wasn't. When we avoid that completely, and when also we seek to avoid thinking that our religion and our faith are simply things that apply inwardly in our own spirits, where we close the doors, would if possible bring down shutters over the glass doors and simply be alone with one another and alone with our God, then reality can break through.

I think there are three things which we need to rediscover and which Paul was pointing the people in Ephesus towards. What did he say: "With deep roots and strong foundations maybe you'll be strong to grasp with all God's people what is the breadth and length and depth and height of the love of Christ and to know it though it is beyond knowledge." He's saying – Take an enormously deep breath. Don't be afraid to lift your eyes. Don't be afraid to move. Don't be afraid to confront the total situation in the face.

I think we have to discover in Christendom again, first of all, the dimension of the universal. That means that we start, as always or (as this may be dishonest because we don't always start here) we start as we should with the very Cross of Christ himself at the very heart of human experience, at the very centre of human history. For there was something quite universal. It's not just for Jews. It's not just for Romans. It's not just for people of a distance century and a past generation. It transcends all these categories. People may find the church divisive and exclusive. They don't find Christ so. They may find the church as being most effective from one standpoint and in one period, but the love of God is wider than the measure of man's mind. Some of us are terribly guilty of expressing our own exclusiveness, almost out of a kind of modesty, as to whom the Christian faith can be for. That there are classes of people, types of people, whom for some reason we feel that the Christian faith, as seen in the Christian church, cannot really be for – and because we sometimes think that, they sometimes think it too. Because they're too young, or too old, or too emancipated or too foreign or too feckless or too poor or too affluent, or too something. And that's always a very wicked thing to say, even if we would never quite get round to saying it in words.

It is for everybody, whether they believe or not. O come all ye faithless. Its measure of love, goodwill and concern has to go so far beyond its own doors, beyond the normal circumference of what Christianity and Christian people are supposed to be, that it extends at least as much, and even more, to those who within our own society not just profess no religion but profess other deeply felt religions in this multi-cultural, pluriform society we live in. We need the dimension of the universal, and there is no aspect of human life and of corporate social experience to which the Gospel itself is not relevant. Wherever you are, in King Charles Street, or Downing Street, or the City Chambers, or in our own homes, the Gospel has a word to speak.

We also need to rediscover, I think, in Christendom, the dimension of the existential, one of these nice, question begging words but a useful one all the same. What I mean is that we need to be at the grass roots of where people's real concern is and where the fact of Christianity is. How often do we let people get away with, and let ourselves get away with, say "I'm not the praying type?" "I'm not really the worshipping type." "I come to the candlelight service at Christmas but I'm not your church sort of person." "I'm not the Women's Guild type, don't look at me."

There are so many people who speak in this way, people with a passion about things which are absolutely central to the human condition. People who are concerned about housing and about marriages and about political and social issues, about education and about Scotland. The things that people care most deeply about. The things that people ought to care most deeply about. The things that people would like to be involved in, if they had the energy, are religious issues, all of them. The insights of Christian truth are relevant to them all. So, we don't close the doors upon the world outside but allow the world outside to hammer in upon us but we also pass it on, as it were, in prayer to God. We find a sense of balance, a sense of perspective, and so we're not ashamed to speak of, and to speak before God of, the matters which oppress a whole society and a whole nation and our own lives.

There is no Christian gospel for men and women that is not concerned with the things that men and women agonize over and are dismayed by and are made joyful by. We can't say forget about the real world and let me give you good news about something you wouldn't ever think about if the thoughts weren't put into your head in church. For the hungry man, the Gospel may come first as food. For the lonely woman, as friendship. For the self-seeking negotiator, as the demand for human justice; and to the man whose wind is set fair, as ultimate responsibility before an eternal God. The deep things of human living, the experiences, the fears that we may hardly be able to articulate upon our lips but which may often surprisingly be printed upon our faces, these things are within the compass of Christian faith. When you find the sermon going on a bit, or when you find the prayers in church to be irrelevant to anything you are concerned about, then dare to switch off sometimes, move your own lips and say, "The things that are my concern today, Lord, are these and these. Answer these, or fit them into the system, or teach me to live with them. But here they are. Don't listen to the minister, Lord, listen to me."

We need to rediscover the dimension of the universal. We need to rediscover the dimension of the existential. I think, also, we have to rediscover in Christendom the dimension of the practical. Some of us have to start again, to learn about God's love in very easy stages and in very short phrases. Many people still are living upon capital invested generations ago and only in this generation (for this the first such generation) has it become not only conventional but wholly respectable to question all the premises that Christian faith is built upon. In this generation, one can go further and it's in terms of human love and human caring that people may discern a goal. To say, because of Jesus Christ and his impulse upon me, I have to do something for you, may be a beginning of faith and may be as much as someone who has been starved of faith may be able to digest. To begin to say, because of Christ, because of his love, because of his interest in me, because of his promised power, I shall today abstain from this one weakness, I shall today treat this one person, whom I have taken for granted, as a human being, with feelings, for the first time.

That may be enough for now. Because of Christ, I shall allow the appeals for money that I see in the papers, the appeals for help for good causes at the cost of maybe one whole evening a week, not pass over my heart and my head but to lodge within my conscience for Jesus' sake. Perhaps we don't always want that Christian faith shall have wide sweeping dimensions but only that it should impinge at one point upon my own conscience and make some small act possible. We maybe don't want our deepest emotions to be brought into the light and under the scrutiny of God. It may be that we don't want the lovely words of Scripture to be debased by the daily usages that seem to speak of our world and our country and our duty. But these are the dimensions that will give Jesus Christ his place in his world, and will give that reality that will make a faith a living and an engrossing thing and the centre of our lives.

And it may be that we do need to observe a little child with no apparent faith but surrounded by love, with no apparent understanding but yet at the heart of a number of people's future plans for their happiness, with only a tiny place within our creation but, we believe, with an enormous place within the heart and love of God. It's only then that we ourselves may be able to lift up our hearts and say, "If God loves him or her, then God loves me too. And if God can work through sacrament, He can work through his word as well, to call me, to send me forth, to give me purpose, meaning, destiny that I would never have found before." When we were without strength, Christ died for us. Let me give you the text once more. Please, if you remember nothing else, remember it: "With deep roots and strong foundations may you be strong to grasp with all God's people what is the breadth and length and depth and height of the love of Christ and to know it, though it is beyond knowledge."

# — THOUGHTS FOR THE DAY —

Whether or not you're a church-goer or believer, you'll probably have heard at least one THOUGHT FOR THE DAY or PRAYER FOR THE DAY in the morning on a BBC radio station. Since the 1930s, some form of reflection from a faith perspective on topical issues has been broadcast to a wide and varied audience. The format (less than 3 minutes live speech) gives 'thinkers' an opportunity to reach many more people than any conventional service allows. So the style and matter of these 'reflections' differ from those used in prayers and sermons.

# WHO CARES?

I don't look like Attila the Hun or Genghis Khan. I'm actually a very humane kind of character, and I am against cruelty. So I have never maltreated an animal by leaving it in an overheated car with the windows closed. I have never maltreated a human being by leaving him in an under-heated room with the windows opened.

Maybe you are like me in that you can't understand why people are cruel, and do the kind of things we read about in the papers. 'Who are these people?' we ask. Would we recognize them? Do they talk like us or do they just gibber? Do they walk normally or do they go sideways on their knuckles?

We know these things happen: the abuse of little children in all sorts of unspeakable ways; the abuse of old people in so-called care, the family pets thrown out of moving cars onto motorways because – well, why? How can people behave like this?

But are we so good? A lot of us would say that we are caring people – but 'caring' is one of the most devalued clichés of our day. What is a caring society or a caring professional? A social worker is not necessarily more caring or less caring than a good plumber or a good motor mechanic who works out of hours to deal with an emergency. A caring society or community don't become so simply by saying they are.

And we can all act out of character. When a marriage breaks up, kindly people can act vindictively, and the more idealized their expectations once were, perhaps the more vindictive they can be. When someone dies and there is money to be looked for, people can behave very oddly.

We say, "I couldn't do that for love nor money" – but it is for love or the denial of love, for money or the lust for money, that people can behave quite out of character, and cruelty and inhumanity can take over.

Statistically, there will be quite a number of us for whom the opportunity for cruelty will be wide open today – and by some of us it will be taken: what you say or don't say over breakfast; a mother at her wits' end over children who drive her out of her mind who decides that a good shaking or a good slapping or worse may not seem to do them much good but might make her feel better. People exulting in their power over someone weaker or more vulnerable at work, someone exasperated with some older person, or in a position to tyrannise some younger person.

"Who could do that? I couldn't do that!" Maybe not, but your life may today be a success or failure because you act with compassion and imagination, or with unfeelingness and cruelty – and that goes for me too. And if I am content in my own comfort, and give not a thought to all those whose lives could be marginally improved if I had the slightest care that they should be, then I too am guilty of cruelty by neglect.

It was Jesus who said to nice people like you and me, "Inasmuch as you have done it to one of the least of these my brothers, you have done it – or failed to do it – to me."

# LOVE IS

The rear window of my car doesn't carry any stickers – apart from one put there by the very good firm who sold me the thing secondhand – and, come to think of it, it's time I was charging them advertising-space for that!

I look at other peoples' stickers, though. The ones that intrigue me are the great range of those that have a crimson heart with 'I' in front of it, meaning 'I love', and then a great variety of alternatives to follow. I wonder who first thought of the idea, and who marketed it – for it's international now – and whether they deservedly made a killing from it. My daughter first saw it in New York – was there an earlier example?

Three I saw last week were these: a glossy car with I LOVE POODLES; one that careened across my bows in a car-park that said I LOVE JESUS; and one with two ladies in it declared I LOVE SOUTH UIST. I don't think there would be a big production run for that one, thought I approve of the sentiment.

Who determines how many of each to produce? And do shopkeepers get a huge album of texts to choose from? And can they simply say 'I'll have 200 I LOVE SCOTLAND, please – or does it come in a kind of package, so that to get 100 GOLDEN LABRADORS one must take 20 I LOVE MILLWALLs, and 5 I LOVE TAX?

I wonder whether in the East of Scotland they market one with a heart followed by two more? Half the football-supporting population might be open to publicising their preferred team!

The nice thing is that there should be so many objects and places that people want to express affection for and not indignation about. They don't say DOWN WITH SO-AND-SO or I DEPLORE SUCH-AND-SUCH.

I remember a cartoon of a member of a religious order in his habit happily carving on an oak tree a pierced heart and the words ANTHONY LOVES EVERYBODY. I suppose you can love everybody . . . but in the end you have to be selective.

I have a rough and ready guide to buying Christmas cards: not to buy charity cards for the prettiness of the picture but for the importance of the cause – so this may mean those working for the mentally-handicapped or those concerned for the conservation of the natural world and endangered species. And you will say – yes – and what about . . . ? And what about . . . ? I agree entirely – but you have to draw a line somewhere.

If you cover your whole windscreen with stickers saying who you love, you won't see very far . . .

# TRUE WISDOM

I listen to the late night news and I hear analysts and experts and economists explaining what is happening in Hong Kong and Wall Street or in Tokyo – and I haven't a clue really what they are talking about. They are talking about forces that are every bit as elemental as winds and tides and hurricanes, and with effects just as dramatic, but all this in the economic field. It seems they use machines that have a kind of life of their own and trigger off the kind of response that they are programmed to do. And I look at the glossy brochure telling me how to sink my nest-egg in British Squilloneum, but I don't really know what is going on. And I'm not sure there is much comfort in suspecting that they don't really know what's going on either. They almost seem, heaven help them, to be as confused as I am. I remember how President Truman longed to meet a one-armed economist, for he said that every economist he knew kept saying "on the one hand and on the other hand".

It's not just that I'm confused about the philosophy and the economics. It's the words. Any reasonable child in Second Year is quite at home now with computers, and quite literally has a whole vocabulary of words which never appeared in my Concise Oxford Dictionary – and I feel somewhat on the sidelines and inadequate in this whole area.

So what do I do? Learn the language? Perhaps I should try. But there may be other languages too.

Some of the most significant people I have known have had none of these abilities. They weren't much use with words, they were fairly inarticulate and they hadn't a clue about finance. They were trusting people – they trusted the experts in any particular field and no doubt they were right to do so. But there was a third world in which they knew instinctively the language of understanding and responsibility and compassion in which they were at home. It may be that some of the bright minds in the world of finance are fairly uneducated when it comes to the particular qualities that make a real society, which are the abilities to relate to other people and to care about other people.

All I am saying is that if you are as confused as I am over finances, your own and other people's, don't be over-clever or over-anxious, and if the opportunity offers in this as in other things, don't be over-selfish. The people who matter most of all are those who don't have much finance at all; and those who are too young to learn a language, or too old to have the chance to learn a new one. But it is by them that any institutions or societies will in the end be judged.

# URBAN TRUTHS

A city is the most fascinating unit in the world we live in – a myriad of people, full of mystery and activity, bright lights and shadows. A great city is alive 24 hours a day; it never sleeps. Rome or Venice, San Francisco or New York – the most stimulating and exciting place to be . . .

A city is the most desolating place on the earth. Calcutta, Djakarta, Mexico City. Grim, hopeless, dehumanizing – the most lonely place on earth to be.

We talk and fantasise about the country – the fields of corn, the lochs and the seaside, but the city is the place to be. That is where the action is, that is where civilization – which just means city life – stands or eventually falls.

Towns want to be known as cities, though it doesn't always work. I like the sound of 'London town' a lot more that I like the sound of the City of London these days. The worst football team I used to watch as a boy was called Edinburgh City, no less – a name to live up to, which I'm afraid it didn't.

I never know what we think of the church having its roots in the countryside. The early church made for the cities – Antioch, Rome, Alexandria: capture the cities and you are there!

Yet we are most ill at ease in cities unless we know them very well. People visualise Jesus as at home in villages and the fields and the hills, but it was the cities he made for, Jerusalem above all. That was where his message had to be heard and obeyed, and, unforgettably, we read that Jerusalem was the city what he looked at and wept over. If Jesus were transplanted into our own day, I don't easily visualize him in the rural areas. I do visualize him as at home in city streets, in concrete canyons, in the marketplaces and shopping centres, and where there is the debris of rubbish and sometimes the debris of people. That is where he would be at home and I think I must say where I believe he is at home – for most people are there and he cared about people passionately, and understood where others didn't. We don't understand cities very much. We know ugly things can happen in them, but after a while the flames die down and the trouble passes and we say "It's over – things are alright again" – but they aren't alright. The reason Jesus wept over the city was that it didn't understand what was happening to itself, what was happening within it.

We still ask when violence breaks out – how can we stop these things happening? We don't ask enough – why do these things happen? We don't perhaps want to understand, for then our own attitudes and values might be called into question.

But until we understand and begin to care, many people in cities will be afraid and will weep, as Jesus wept long ago, and perhaps weeps yet.

# STEP BY STEP

'It"s nice up here," I said, panting a bit, to someone the other day, "Fine view you get." "Yes," said the old person I was visiting, "if it wasn't for the stairs." And I wondered how often I had heard these words during my years as a minister in a city – "IF IT WASN'T FOR THE STAIRS"! Stairs are a means of access; they are also a means of isolation.

Over Christmas, there was a programme of film-clips on one of the channels on the theme of stairways. Good stuff – from the showgirls descending staircases in musicals of the '30s to the nightmarish chases up staircases in Hitchcock climaxes; from comics rolling down them to to swashbuckling swordplay up them. One moment that wasn't used was that epic moment in Stevenson's KIDNAPPED, when David Balfour in the House of Shaws finds in the dark that the staircase is broken – with nothingness beyond it. Stairways are a powerful symbol. The ultimate one in the Bible – the dream of a young man, Jacob, who has left home behind him – no contact now. He is on his own, and he is sleeping rough. In his dream he has a vision of a ladder, or a stairway, set up on earth and reaching to heaven and above it. God, the God of Bethel, and the angels of God move up and down upon it. He knows he need never again be out of communication there.

To be unable to communicate, to make yourself known to anyone, is loneliness and alienation, and in the end the denial of humanity. One of the marks of being human is to be able to communicate realistically with others. And one of the profound descriptions of God in all the great religions, and certainly within Christianity and Judaism, is that he communicates with his creatures: through an inner voice, some would say. Others would want to say through that ultimate human contact which was in Christ – God entering onto our own experience and into our human life.

In our complex world, where you don't have to see someone directly to make contact, or even hear his voice, where communication is sustained through tenuous cables and electric impulses, we realize how vulnerable we are.

Communications are our lifeline, and when they become frayed then wise and responsible people on both sides of the jagged break will be working to mend things. For a society like ours cannot endure for long any kind of breakdown.

Others of us in our daily lives, perhaps most of us, have the task of keeping communications open, using stairways (even if we are peching a bit in the process), and helping others less able to use them, so that the stairs don't become a symbol of isolation but of the continuation of communication without which life is less worth living than it might be.

# PRIDE AND PREJUDICE

I have thought of a good title for a book – *Pride and Prejudice* – how about that? I know that you'd never get a book sold with a title like that. On the other hand, it is original . . . maybe for a study of the attitudes of European nations to each other – or perhaps for a frank autobiography.

Pride is not a bad thing, sometimes – for instance, having a good conceit of yourself. But prejudices are funny things. You and I don't have them but other people do. Have you ever said – no, of course you haven't, but you have heard someone else say about their new neighbours, "Of course, actually they're Pakistani, they're Jewish, they're Londoners, they're Catholics, they're Plymouth Brethren, they're boat-people, etc, etc but I must say they're very pleasant and they keep their children well turned out." And it's that 'but' that betrays. 'They' are different, they don't belong to the minority that is me.

It is national characteristics that show pride and prejudice most. I can think of a good reason for being prejudiced against just about every nation under the sun. That lot – now, they kill small birds by the million, and those folk hog the loungers beside the pool. Or they're beastly to bulls, or they imprison people and beat their feet, or they fought on the wrong side. Or they're too primitive, or too successful.

For my generation it is too easy to keep prejudices going. My generation nurses its history and sometimes its myths; a younger generation may devalue history, may say history is past and it doesn't matter. History IS past, and it DOES matter.

So you don't pretend there was no Auschwitz, no Siam railway, no KGB. But how long do you allow the sins of the fathers to taint the present generations? Some of the Old Testament prophets were very strong on each generation paying for its predecessors' transgressions.

What is most eerie is when people seem to pretend that the past just didn't happen. For the health of this small planet, we have to recognize facts, not forget the past, nor distort or ignore it. Forgiveness is always costly, but over and over again it is the only way forward. Harbouring prejudice, on the other hand, is easy, and obliterating or rewriting the past can be convenient. Facing the past, recognizing it for what it is and offering and accepting forgiveness may be the only way forward in our own relationships, and for nations too.

# NOW WHAT?

Mid-January is a kind of limbo period. Last Christmas is long gone. And the next break, Easter, is somewhere over the horizon. Yet Christmas was real in its satisfaction or disappointment, in its strange bitter-sweet of expectation fulfilled or denied. The great thing about the Christian year is that it focuses your attention on one point and keeps it from wandering all over the place. The weeks of Advent sharpen the hopes and apprehensions for all the futures that are always there. At Christmas, the hopes and fears of ALL the years converge. And we revive the sense that God was – is – here on a one-way ticket irrevocably into all the pedestrian-ness of routine and the ordinariness of things, so that WE don't have to spell out to him in words of one syllable what it feels like to be human.

And then he gives a tracing of a pilgrimage which is our OWN pilgrimage through life, the growing awareness that is our own experience, which is not always springtime. The shadows will lengthen and the evening will come – and it is not for all a peaceful twilight. In many lives there comes suddenly the comfortless stress and tension of defeat and death. And it seems, at first, light years from the Nativity stories we were singing about so recently. And then we see that it was there all the time – a sword, said the messenger at the beginning, shall pierce your own soul.

The fact is that it is always Christmas. It is always Easter. The shadow of the Cross falls over all our living. It is just that at certain moments we turn the searchlight on one or other of these events in order to give them full value, because each is complete and absolute in itself. Life and death and pain, things present, things to come – each has to be given its full weight. We have to examine them one by one. And we learn to say – the poignancy of the Incarnation is in the Cross that will follow. And the Cross would be intolerable to contemplate if it were not that we have sneaked a look at the last chapter and seen that the empty tomb is yet to come. Not the last chapter either – there are appendices to follow: our present life which is compounded of a world shot through with glory and achievement and victory and unimaginable pain. Life which at first seems to stretch into the future soon begins to be foreshortened, so that the teenager begins to panic at the onset of middle age, and the elderly wonder what happened to all those years. Where was 2000, let alone 1990?

The last chapter too we sometimes catch a glimpse of, for that is the ultimate, when the problems are resolved, the solutions made evident, and we marvel that we hadn't seen it all the time. The events all come in succession, but every one is contemporary. Christ did not only come, he comes. He did not only suffer, he suffers. He did not once rise from the death of the hopes of many, he does yet – each returning day.

Lord, help us today to understand that segment of our lives that today will bring, and to see beyond its radiance or its somberness. Help us to see that joy and pain, defeat and victory are part of the very experience of our God, and that through them all we may come closer to him.

# IMAGINE

The images that we have of God are sometimes curious and disturbing, and often childish. Not our fault, really. We have inherited them from childhood pictures, from age-old tradition. In most of the great religions, the two most telling names for God are Lord (which suggests power and sovereignty) or Father (which suggests care and responsibility and wisdom and discipline and abiding love). Yet 'Lord' can suggest mediaeval sovereignty enthroned, which is not how we see power today, and the Father-figure is more often a grandfather-figure – not the vital, youthful, energetic, creative, active sort of father so familiar to our own society.

We live in an age of visual images. What is your image of God and the things he does? What are the parallels you can point to? For some, the idea of God means an inaugurator of many things that he then has no further interest in – as it were, clipping ribbons to open something, smashing bottles against a hull to launch something, or signing contracts to set things in motion – and then walking away. God as overseer or maintenance engineer, clock winder or piano tuner. Or as a foreman keeping an eye on productivity – or an emergency resource ("in straits a present aid"), flying doctor, close circuit TV scanner, ombudsman, director of studies, rich uncle, or the ultimate mother figure, or a nightmare father abusing his own creations – and at the end of the day, the presenter of the classified results.

These are twentieth-century images. None of us would consciously subscribe to anything so naïve, but to get a consistent twentieth-century picture we may have to go back through tradition to discover what men and women once claimed (as some still do): God as wholly involved in the daily life of plant and animal and crystal, as in the Bible the psalmist saw; God as involved in the pressures of the market-place, as in the Bible Amos saw; involved in the aspirations and heartbreaks of family life, as in the Bible Hosea saw; involved in the places where statesmen meet, blueprints are drawn up in directors' suites and senate rooms, as in the Bible Isaiah saw. God as involved in the excitement of technological society, as in the Bible Ezekiel saw, for God was in the wheels; or involved in the fears and hopes of a new millennium and of an imminent apocalypse, as the writers of the books of Daniel and Revelation saw. And targeting with concern and compassion the poor and the helpless and the voiceless, as the writers of the Bible from beginning to end were obliged to recognize. The images can be confusing. Perhaps we are best to go back to where we began: to the sovereignty and fatherhood of God. Others have found this sufficient, and so may we.

Almighty God, sovereign Lord, loving Father, we offer ourselves today to your caring, to your governing, to your direction, to your blessing.

# EXTRA-ORDINARY

The cotoneaster outside my kitchen wall is a thing of beauty and excitement just now – a blaze of red berries. It has been so for months. The weather hasn't been cold enough for the birds to come and strip them, though they're welcome to do so when the time comes. I can't say that it speaks to me of anything profound other than its beauty, which is enough, and I'm thankful for it on a grey day. But I recall how so many people are on record as having looked at something very ordinary whose beauty might have been overlooked and found something unimaginable.

Jeremiah did when he saw fumes coming from a cooking-pot with the wind blowing from the north, for he realized something was brewing; and when he saw the early flowering of the almond. I suppose Moses did when he saw a bush aflame with colour in the desert and something was triggered within him which he knew to be nothing less than the voice of the living God.

The New Testament, of course, is supremely a picture-book of the Gospel. Jesus was a master not just of the one-liner – and the Gospels are full of these, many of which we can quote without necessarily knowing their source – but the quick sketch that brought situations and people to life. Some of them are like film-clips with the ending cut off so that you have to provide your own ending. Some of them are simply dramatic illustrations that make the Gospels a sheer picture-book such as no other religious work has ever been. And just as in modern book production you sometimes get all the photographs gathered together at one point in the text, so the Gospel writers in some cases had the idea of gathering up a lot of these pictures and placing them side by side – and the effect is all the greater.

So you can almost hear Jesus casting about in his mind how to illustrate effectively what he wants to say. The kingdom of heaven – what on earth is it like? It's like a sower casting his seed by hand – broadcasting, we would say. Sometimes it works, and more often it turns off completely. What else? Well, it's like a field of high quality seeds with weeds growing in it too. And he looks around at his audience to see if that strikes a light, and he sees the glazed, earnest look that most preachers know only too well. No? Oh well, it's like – the kingdom is like – a tiny grain of seed with incredible potential; it's like a woman mixing leaven in her bread, creating energy and growth where it wasn't before. What else? It's like a man stubbing his toe against a treasure in someone else's field and he knows he has at any cost to get that treasure for himself. The kingdom is like a fisherman's net, a net that gathers all the good fish AND the uneatable fish, and they have to be sorted out. It's like any of these things, all of these things. Perhaps we have to learn to recognize the images of God and his kingdom, and to interpret them. They may be on a television screen; they may be in people whom we meet in the ordinary course of events. And the world of God may come quite compellingly and dramatically in either of these.

Make us alert, Lord, to see you and to hear you in the ordinary things and in the unexpected things, and to respond as we should.

# A NEW DAY

This is not a switching-on time for prayer, really. But it is an important time as the day begins. It is a time for coming alive, facing the prospect, shaking off the darkness – perhaps exorcising some of the goblins that have emerged during the dark hours, when things get out of perspective, and sending them scuttling back to their holes.

A good time, this, to pray. But I suppose as the earth wheels round, prayer is simply continuous worldwide. There is not a moment when the air is not sizzling and twanging with thanksgiving, appeal, anxiety, commitment – a kind of shimmering haze of prayer over the planet directed outward from ourselves, from myriads of people affirming that the world's life and wellbeing depend on God. There's a hymn that says it exactly – a fine morning hymn if you cut off the first verse: "As o'er each continent and island/The dawn leads on another day/The voice of prayer is never silent". So some of us are revving up for a day that is already underway. Others are saying a quick word for those who have started out: "Lord, keep him safe on the motorway. It's Friday and he's tired. Help him to remember his lanes and to be patient on the slip road." Or "Bless the driver of his train this morning and the signalmen on duty."

Others of us reflecting on what must shortly be done: "How soon can I phone her and break the news? Will 7.30 be too early or too late? Lord, prepare her for what I'm going to tell her, and prepare me for saying it." Or even: "Right, Lord, this is it. This is the day. The night staff is going off. They've moved my bed to be near the door. I've been shaved and washed and I'm ready. Into the surgeon's hands I commend my body. Into your hands, Lord, I commend my spirit."

Yes, prayer this morning takes many forms. Thanksgiving, expectancy, exhilaration, foreboding. "This is the Lord's doing, but nothing is beyond his power and his love." And we slot in our own prayer as if there was no other one, and all around was silence; as if we really matter – and we believe we do. Father, hear the multitude of prayers that rise to you, the father of us all. Lord, hear our prayer and let our cry come up to you.